JAN FABRE

THE SERVANT OF BEAUTY

*Seven monologues
for the theatre*

JAN FABRE
THE SERVANT OF BEAUTY
Seven monologues for the theatre

*Edited and Foreword by
Frank Hentschker*

MARTIN E. SEGAL
THEATRE CENTER

*Martin E. Segal Theatre Center Publications
New York*
© 2010

Library of Congress Cataloging-in-Publication Data

Fabre, Jan, 1958-
[Plays. English. Selections]
The servant of beauty : 7 monologues for the theatre / Jan Fabre ; edited and foreword by Frank Hentschker.
    p. cm.
ISBN 978-0-9846160-1-5
1. Fabre, Jan, 1958---Translations into English. I. Hentschker, Frank. II. Title.
PT6466.16.A3A2 2010
839.31'264--dc22
                2010051479

Edited by Frank Hentschker
Cover design, typography, and design by Marcel Lennartz (monsieurmoire.com)
Production supervision and copy-editing by Katrien Bruyneel
and Miet Martens, Troubleyn

© 2010 Martin E. Segal Theatre Center
Frank Hentschker, Executive Director
Daniel Gerould, Director of Academic Affairs and Publications
Jan Stenzel, Director of Administration

TABLE OF CONTENTS

FOREWORD

Jan Fabre's anthology, *The Servant of Beauty - Seven Monologues for the Theatre*, confronts the reader with selected dramatic works ranging from 1975 *(she was and she is, even ...)* until 2010 *(we need heroes now)*. With this collection, Fabre, a Flemish-Belgian titan in the global world of contemporary performance and art, establishes himself as an auteur du théâtre. His *écriture plurielle*, works and monologues for the theatre, are hypertexts for the contemporary stage in the slip stream of Heiner Müller. Following the footsteps of his mythical hero Heracles, perhaps better known as Hercules, his Roman name, Fabre attempts "the rescue attempt" proposed by theatre theorist Peter Szondi: to liberate drama, chained to the rocks of realism, commercialism and bland, non-descript entertainment. But Fabre claims dual roles for the contemporary artist: the eternally wounded and chained Prometheus, who stole the fire from the Gods and has to suffer the consequences; as well as Hercules, the Titan's liberator, who killed "heaven's winged hound" (Percy Bysshe Shelley), the eagle that tortured Prometheus. It is Fabre's belief that inhuman suffering and heroic rescue go hand in hand, that they are together the source of artistic creation, a daily practice without salvation. According to Fabre, the artist, writing "with the blood of roses," *(we need heroes now)* is mocked and pushed to the edges of society like a dog on a highway and yet is also the only figure strong enough to endure such suffering. Only the artist, challenging the gods again and again, can honor what Prometheus has stolen as mankind's most heavenly gifts: light, fire and all the arts of civilization, including writing, science, art, architecture, mathematics, agriculture, medicine and more. The following are the only four lines the Hero speaks in *we need heroes now*, (2010)

You will never close the wound
out of which beauty seeps
Let my red flowers bloom
Until I'm empty

The Prometheus myth is central to Fabre's work and to his ideas about the role of the artist in society. The title of his 2011 work, *Prometheus-Landscape II*, is like his *Prometheus Landscape I* (1988), a reference to Heiner Müller and his *Medeamaterial Landschaft mit Argonauten*. Müller's text is a collage, an arrangement of material used to paint over T. S. Elliot's *The Waste Land*. Fabre's work also seems affiliated to Müller's *Hamletmaschine*. "I am half organ and half machine," screams the protagonist in Fabre's 1996 *little body on the wall*. The 1988 *Prometheus Landscape I* was presented in Berlin at the same festival where Heiner Müller and Robert Wilson worked together on *The Forest*. Fabre's 1997 Prometheus-inspired collaboration with Belgian choreographer Wim Vandekeybus, *little body on the wall*, toured for two years around the world. In this production, Vandekeybus, a former member of the Fabre company and now one of the best European dancers and choreographers of his generation, appeared bound on stage, immobilized, with microphone cable glued to his hands as a new-media Prometheus on an inter-media stage, screaming in defiance of the gods: "Little body on the wall, who has the most beautiful blood corpuscles of them all?"

The performance text for *Prometheus-Landscape II*, created in collaboration with Jeroen Olyslaegers, differs slightly from the Fabre text we need heroes now presented in this collection. Fabre adopted the words we need heroes now from a poster he saw at Ground Zero in New York City just after the 9/11 tragedy.

Fabre's monologues are postdramatic monodramas. Monodrama is theatre, in which the drama is created and acted by a single person. Nikolai Evreinov, the early twentieth-century Russian theorist of monodrama points, out that an audience sees a character from a single, subjective point-of-view. The author serves as *dramatis figura*, protagonist of the dramatic world, but we experience that world through the psyche of a central character. Jean-Jacques Rousseau's *Pygmalion*, Percy Bysshe Shelley's *Prometheus Unbound*, Schubert's *Winterreise*, Mayakovsky's *Mayakovsky: A Tragedy*, Karl Kraus's *The Last Days of Mankind*, Samuel Beckett's *Happy Days*, Heiner Müller's *Hamletmaschine* can be considered examples of monodrama. Like the Greek myths, monodrama has been with us since the birth of theatre 2500 years ago. The actor Thespis is credited with inventing this form of theatre with his revolutionary idea of stepping out of the chorus as a single performer and performing plays with several characters as one-man shows, indicating different characters with different linen masks and costumes.

A postdramatic monodrama, however, goes even further: a total theatre, created and performed by a single person; where every word, thought, idea, sound, light cue, set feature and stage direction emanates from a single psyche in the urgent attempt to communicate directly with the audience. Robert Wilson's *Solo Performance*, (1969), Fabre's *she was and she is even...* (1975) and Spalding Gray's *Swimming to Cambodia* (1985) are examples of such postdramatic monodramas.

Fabre could also be seen as an unorthodox, *fin-de-millennium* European symbolist. In Belgium Symbolism has deep roots as seen in the work of artists like the playwright, poet and essayist Maurice Maeterlinck, poet Albert Giraud who wrote the libretto for Schönberg's *Pierrot Lunaire*, the Flemish painter and printmaker James Ensor, and the Surrealist René Magritte.

In Fabre's trilogy, also included in this anthology, *the emperor of loss, the king of plagiarism* and *the servant of beauty*, he again places himself and the attendant drama of the artist in search of a place in contemporary society on the stage. Revealing himself as a Symbolist, Fabre paints his own self-portrait as a clown, an angel, a king, a puppeteer. Taking on the mask of the clown, Fabre's very own version of Giraud's *Pierrot Lunaire*, he accepts the aesthetic of failure as key to the process of making art. On stage in the king of plagiarism, we see stones that symbolize Einstein (science), Wittgenstein (philosophy), Gertrude Stein (art) and Frankenstein (artificial intelligence), all lined up before a failed operation. (Marry Shelley, the wife of Percy Bysshe Shelley, gave her Frankenstein novel the subtitle A Modern Prometheus.) As expressed by Luk Van den Dries, who observes Fabre's work closely: "Jan Fabre's visual world is a hall of mirrors. This applies not least to the metaphorical images and accompanying characters in his plays, such as the double, the twin, the parrot, the monkey and so on. These characters and metaphors are often in search of an identity and have come to the conclusion that their identity is 'borrowed,' or is multiplying. In each case this identity is rarely unambiguous."

Hans-Thies Lehman, who coined the term Postdramatic Theatre, and who is currently involved in his own research on tragedy, wrote of the Belgian: "Fabre's work is essentially tragic – and modern tragedy borders of course on the grotesque, on satire, on the sinister. But whereas in traditional drama it used to matter what happened between bodies, in post-dramatic theatre, it matters what happens to the body itself."

It is my hope that with this publication of a second volume of Fabre's writing, directors and performers will be inspired to use Fabre's work for their own successful attempts at failure, endure the suffering and the liberation of Prometheus, and experience being the clown, the angel, the king, the marionette and other players from Fabre's dramatic universe.

- Fabre, Jan. Seven Works for the Theatre. New York, 2009.
- Lehman, Hans-Thies. Postdramatic Theatre. London, 2006.
- Van den Dries, Luk. Corpus Jan Fabre: Observations of a Creative Process. Gent, 2004.
- Evreinov, Nikolai. "Introduction to Monodrama. [1909]" In Senelick, Laurence, ed.
- Russian Dramatic Theory from Pushkin to the Symbolists: An Anthology. Texas, 1981.
  Taroff, Kurt. "The Mind's Stage: Monodrama as Historical Trend and Interpretive Strategy." Graduate Center, City University of New York, 2005.
- http://www.troubleyn.be

WE NEED HEROES NOW

Jan Fabre, 2010

English translation by Gregory Ball

Dedicated to my heroine

Sources / notes

(1) On 12 September 2001, in front of Ground Zero in New York, a group of people were photographed holding a banner saying WE NEED HEROES NOW.

(2) Lao-Tse, Tao Te Ching, text 66

(3) F. Nietzsche

(4) Like a true coward I used everything that I could find about heroes

PLAY FOR 2 VOICES

For the first time we write
with red flowers
WE NEED HEROES NOW [1]

In a world
where chronic instability
repeatedly degenerates
into gruesome acts of violence
on a gigantic scale

It is also a world
that offers infinite opportunities
to our hero
Where is our hero?
I can smell him
Where is the tempting presence which
armed with red flowers
goes into battle
He knows the violence of aesthetics
and the aesthetics of violence
Beauty breeds heroism
FUCK YOU, SIGMUND FREUD

Are we desperate?
Do we crave a seducer
with brilliant acting talent?
Do we yearn for courage
incarnate with a theatrical heroism?
I ask you again!
For the second time
Where is our hero?
Where is he!
That's right, it is a man
And even if it were a woman
she would have to wear men's clothes
to enter the pantheon of heroes
FUCK YOU SIGMUND FREUD
FUCK YOU KAREN HORNEY
FUCK YOU MARY AINSWORTH
AND FUCK YOU ANNA FREUD

Are we desperate?
Do we crave a champion
with an infinite fighting spirit ?
Do we yearn for a rebel
with an intimidating bravura?
I ask you again!
For the third time

Where is our hero?
Who will give his all for us
Even his life
To make his uniqueness count
To give his mortality
worth and meaning
and to escape from oblivion
FUCK YOU SIGMUND FREUD
FUCK YOU KAREN HORNEY
FUCK YOU MARY AINSWORTH
FUCK YOU ANNA FREUD
AND FUCK YOU ALFRED ADLER

Are we desperate?
Do we long for a protector
who is genuinely exalted?
Do we yearn for a saviour
with an intoxicating charm?
I ask you again!
For the fourth time
Where is our hero?
Who as an ordinary man
dares to oppose giants
Who with subversive and ironic humour
pokes fun at the extreme
and dangerous authority
FUCK YOU SIGMUND FREUD
FUCK YOU KAREN HORNEY
FUCK YOU MARY AINSWORTH
FUCK YOU ANNA FREUD
FUCK YOU ALFRED ADLER
AND FUCK YOU ERIK ERIKSON

Are we desperate?
Do we long for a bearer
of archaic nobleness
with a stirring oratorical talent?
Do we yearn for a revolutionary partisan
with unshakable courage?
I ask you again!
For the fifth time
Where is our hero?
Who is willing to totally
discard his humanness
and become entirely animal
Who has a name like a spell
with a magical effect
Who is always faithful

to himself
and his principles
FUCK YOU SIGMUND FREUD
FUCK YOU KAREN HORNEY
FUCK YOU MARY AINSWORTH
FUCK YOU ANNA FREUD
FUCK YOU ALFRED ADLER
FUCK YOU ERIK ERIKSON
AND FUCK YOU KURT LEWIN

Are we desperate?
Do we long for a thrilling outsider
with unbridled flair
Do we yearn for a free wanderer
whose choice is absolute
I ask you again!
For the sixth time
Where is our hero?
Who knows the value of speed
and can appear there
where no one expects it
Shocking and awe-inspiring
like a supernatural figure
Who can demoralise the opposition
and give us, allies, fresh courage
I saw him briefly... I think
FUCK YOU SIGMUND FREUD
FUCK YOU KAREN HORNEY
FUCK YOU MARY AINSWORTH
FUCK YOU ANNA FREUD
FUCK YOU ALFRED ADLER
FUCK YOU ERIK ERIKSON
FUCK YOU KURT LEWIN
AND FUCK YOU CARL JUNG

Are we desperate?
Do we long for a visionary warrior
With a compelling ambition, fame
Do we yearn for a true knight
from days long gone
with a pure intensity
I ask you again!
For the seventh time
Where is our hero?
Who is a legend
Someone whose self-made myth
is an invention of impressive grandeur
A man who occupies an important place

in our imagination
FUCK YOU SIGMUND FREUD
FUCK YOU KAREN HORNEY
FUCK YOU MARY AINSWORTH
FUCK YOU ANNA FREUD
FUCK YOU ALFRED ADLER
FUCK YOU ERIK ERIKSON
FUCK YOU KURT LEWIN
FUCK YOU CARL JUNG
AND FUCK YOU IVAN PAVLOV

Are we desperate?
Do we long for a glorious resistance fighter
With a glimmer of magnificence
Do we yearn for a pacifist who fights
with divine stupidity
I ask you again!
For the eight time!
Where is our hero?
Who has shaped himself
through the past
And who will determine the shape
of our future
Who we want to worship
and revere
I feel him
He has the aura
of a near-human tragedy
FUCK YOU SIGMUND FREUD
FUCK YOU KAREN HORNEY
FUCK YOU MARY AINSWORTH
FUCK YOU ANNA FREUD
FUCK YOU ALFRED ADLER
FUCK YOU ERIK ERIKSON
FUCK YOU KURT LEWIN
FUCK YOU CARL JUNG
FUCK YOU IVAN PAVLOV
AND FUCK YOU ALFRED BINET

Are we desperate?
Do we long for a founder of a new academy
with the natural quality of a leader
Do we yearn for an energetic young dictator
with wisdom way beyond his years
If you want to lead the people, you have to follow them [2]
I ask you again!
For the ninth time
Where is our hero?

The God-made aristocrat
The history of the world
is his biography
Where is he?
Has he fled once again
with the agonizing illusion
of a defeated idealist?
FUCK YOU SIGMUND FREUD
FUCK YOU KAREN HORNEY
FUCK YOU MARY AINSWORTH
FUCK YOU ANNA FREUD
FUCK YOU ALFRED ADLER
FUCK YOU ERIK ERIKSON
FUCK YOU KURT LEWIN
FUCK YOU CARL JUNG
FUCK YOU IVAN PAVLOV
FUCK YOU ALFRED BINET
AND FUCK YOU WILLIAM JAMES

Are we desperate?
Do we long for a philosopher-pirate
with a vulgar yet enchanting character
Do we yearn for a universal donor
with his own rhetoric
with a desire to destroy
to change
to create something new [3]
I ask you again!
For the tenth time
Where is our hero?
I see the traces
of his life fluids
For his enemies he is an obvious target
Is he hurt?
For us, disciples
A fantasy
Is he wounded?
FUCK YOU SIGMUND FREUD
FUCK YOU KAREN HORNEY
FUCK YOU MARY AINSWORTH
FUCK YOU ANNA FREUD
FUCK YOU ALFRED ADLER
FUCK YOU ERIK ERIKSON
FUCK YOU KURT LEWIN
FUCK YOU CARL JUNG
FUCK YOU IVAN PAVLOV
FUCK YOU ALFRED BINET
FUCK YOU WILLIAM JAMES

AND FUCK YOU CARL ROGERS
AND FUCK YOU ALL SECOND RATE,
THIRD RATE AND FOURTH RATE
PSYCHO-FUCKERS

Are we desperate?
Do we long for a symbolic prophet
with ancient worship
Do we yearn for an altruistic
dandy-poet
with a romantic soul
I ask you again!
For the eleventh time
Where is our hero?
That triumphant hero
is a holy martyr
He doesn't conquer
He arrives
He is the bringer of the colour of freedom
And embodies the tragic beauty
of defeat
He will die
but he won't be dead
Shall I staunch
and tend to his wounds?
I hear him

HERO
You will never close the wound
out of which beauty seeps
Let my red flowers bloom
until I'm empty

Are we desperate?
Do we long for an authentic creative being
with a genuine belief
in the lie of the imagination
Do we yearn for an artistic model
with the unscrupulous power
to transform
I ask you again! JESUS CHRIST!
For the twelfth time
Where is our hero?
Where is our fine crystal vase?
In which we can arrange our red roses
To adorn our home
To admire our love

One last time we write
With the blood of roses
WE NEED HEROES NOW

◆

SHE WAS AND SHE IS, EVEN...

Jan Fabre, 1975

English translation by Gregory Ball

For Liliane van H.

Sources / notes

Inspired by Marcel Duchamp's La mariée mise à nue par ses célibataires, même (Le Grand Verre)

MONOLOGUE FOR A YOUNG (MARY'S ASCENSION) WOMAN

(pleasure, enjoyment, laughter)
Where are we?
What's going on here, if anything's going on?
Let's gradually go up...
My only function is to make love
I'm no good for anything else
Should I be?
My only function is to make love
  again
and again
and again
and again
and again
and again
and again
in all kinds of guises
My only function is to make love
Although there are men who ardently desire
to hear my confession
And boys who will steal anything for me
from supermarkets
And there are men in uniforms who never
want to fine me and want to put me under state security
And there are men
who give me a free quote for
my coffin
Men
who wish to serve my imaginative wishes hand and foot
Men with difficult jobs
who want to do difficult things
for me
There are even men
who clear and wipe the table
I sit at, under the parasol
shaded from bright sunlight
While I see men controlling the trains
and occasionally they make them
crash for me
To make me laugh
Sweet, isn't it?
(laughs with delight)
The poor souls
The game decides
chance decides
which colour I shall show them
Time will do its work
Red lead
and nature's oxidation

is what's needed every hour
Parasol
parasol
parasol
parasol
beneath dust
coloured by all their fuss
Poor souls
But they're so spontaneous
They grind on and on
They taste of milk chocolate
They grind on and on
I've licked it, but not bitten
the trace they leave
and leave behind
The temptation
hard to resist
Nothing works the way you think
it should work
The chocolate that comes from
I don't know where
and yet hard to resist
Are these men soldiers too
or are they hairdressers
The bayonet has X-shaped scissors
What complex creatures
those poor souls
A little to the left, I think...
(closes her eyes)
From here to eternity
   again
and again
and again
and again
and again
and again
and again
jerking forward
and backward
The poor souls
A sledge underneath them
or a slider
a sort of trolley on rails
equipped
for even more fuss
(slowly opens her eyes)
Optician's eyewitnesses
far right, I think

Mirror, mirror on the wall
Who is the loveliest of us all?
It's the other side
The past
I know about it
All these complicated methods
The methods of their seduction
They look at me with one eye, close up,
for almost an hour
Peeping Toms
with furtive eyes
waiting for the undressing of myself
No bared self
but a fresh widow
Tch, tch, tch, the poor souls
The poor souls, inferior in every way
to me
The poor souls, even their desire for me
is started up by myself
The poor souls, that I so desire
I order
the poor souls obey
All explanations are too one-sided
and nothing can be denied
I follow them
from the one astonishing step to the next
They're incredibly inventive
Not film stills
They're stupefying
I can smell them
with my eyes closed, even
Luminous gas
And they're singing
a sort of male lament
The melancholy sounds originate from
From here to eternity
   again
and again
and again
and again
and again
and again
and again
jerking forwards
and backwards
Live slowly
Vicious circle
Horizontal

The track to the buffer
life's waste
cheap construction
tin
rope and iron wire

Eccentric wooden pulleys
monotonous flywheel
beer professor
They always repeat these painful words
until they fuse into a single point
Nothing is odder than it's truth
They change
as always
A real metamorphosis of long, thin needles
to prick me, who knows...
They become frozen little gas hearts
that are lighter than air
But before they rise up they are filtered
Censorship?
I see... they are getting dizzy, but it's only temporary
and they're losing their individuality, and that's for good
Everything's unclear and not visible
What adventurers
From here to eternity
  again
and again
and again
and again
and again
and again
and again
The last four are full of filth
jerking forwards
and backwards
The gas hearts have turned into drops
They're dripping hearts
Everything's unclear and not visible
So much dripping
Poor souls
Everything's unclear and not visible according to
the optician's eyewitnesses
Immediately below it
Now
The dripping hearts fall blindly
in love
(she roars with laughter)
No, the dripping hearts are thrown

blindly at me at terrible speed
through the midst of the optician's eyewitnesses
How rude
What a nerve!
Defying a dream
I'm everything to them
and everything here is vague and unreal like in a dream
But everything is possible
because the elements of desire
are coming this way at a terrible speed
At this lucrative moment the dripping hearts
turn into an explosive liquid
How exciting!
The dripping hearts, explosively on their way
Arrival in my spattering splash region
What else could I call it?
Little engines on their way
always on the way
From here to eternity
  again
and again
and again
and again
and again
and again
and again
jerking forwards
and backwards
Poor souls
Then they're out for the count
Tch, tch, tch, oh the poor souls

When, carefully
very carefully and slowly we go up even higher...
Almost
but not entirely
A sort of timid strength
is my reservoir of love petrol
The dividing line between above and below
is my desire-magnet
Would poor souls like these
understand passionate words
Right above the reservoir is an engine
with very weak cylinders
that's connected to my skeleton
The soft seat
the softest system in my all-controlling fantasy
Mirror, mirror on the wall

Who is the loveliest of them all?
The back
and I see the front
　again
and again
and again
and again
and again
and again
and again
jerking forwards
and backwards
What nerves of steel
to constantly undergo this
The nerve centre of my desire
My fantasy sees the sum of the exquisite vibrations
A cloud, immeasurable
with open windows
strong winds
air valves
the halo

Below my halo
Up a little more...
Nine shots from a toy pistol with
matchstick bullets
Colours and times
by chance
The shots will bring the poor souls'
explosive dripping hearts under my control
Time does its best
on the way to the boxing match
The dripping hearts do their best too
Drip, drip, and drip so many more times
All that dripping
(laughs)
See them at it so impetuously
The boxing match, invisible
and never completed
is electricity
The electric undressing should ignite
my love petrol in my engine
I'm a passive witness of my own
undressing
I'm waiting
as always
I'm waiting, in vain
but excited

My engine has very weak cylinders
as I've already said

I fulfil my purpose
Very slowly, but very, very carefully
up a little bit more...
I do my best and make sparks
through my desire magnet
to my engine with its weak cylinders
But I think my engine really has very weak cylinders
From here to eternity
   again
and again
and again
and again
and again
and again
and again
jerking forwards
and backwards
Seven days
Seven moons
Seven men...
eternally on the way from desire to fulfilment
Poor souls, keep it up

Machines, machines
Blossoms have to blossom
consenting, desiring
and copying
ANDY

◆

ETANT DONNÉS

Jan Fabre, 2000

English translation by Gregory Ball

© Wonge Bergmann, 2004

For Els Deceukelier

Sources / notes

Inspired by Duchamp, a biography by Calvin Tomkin

(1) Duchamp uses the word 'bricoleur', roughly equivalent in modern terms to a 'DIY enthusiast' or a 'handyman'.

A MONOLOGUE FOR A WOMAN AND HER VAGINA

SHE
Since the summer of 69
between
10 o'clock in the morning and 5 o'clock in the evening
I have lain on my back
with my legs open

Wait a moment
Wait a moment
Wait a moment
A moment, wait

I lie on my back
with my legs open
behind an old worn-out door
In silence
I remain silent
And just look
In the door at eye level
there are two cracks or are they
two holes?

HER VAGINA
PEEPHOLES FOR PEEPING TOMS

SHE
To peep at me

HER VAGINA
To peep at who?

SHE
Outside the set hours
I wander round a bit
and occasionally talk
to anyone who wants to listen
Perhaps the bachelors listen
Sometimes I can smell them
Where are you?

HER VAGINA
To peep at who?

SHE
I lie on my back
with my legs open
Then no one can see
my beautiful expressive face

Isn't that a shame?
Then no one can see
my wavy blond hair
Isn't that a shame?

HER VAGINA
To peep at who?

SHE
Now you can admire me in full
Where are you?
Sometimes I miss them
Then I look
until they see me

HER VAGINA
To peep at who?

SHE
Who am I?
They know who I am

HER VAGINA
To peep at who?

SHE
I lie on my back
with my legs open
I'm timeless
Perhaps even
The origin of the world?

HER VAGINA
To peep at who?

SHE
I'm a painting
I'm a sculpture
I'm an installation
I'm the performance

HER VAGINA
You are a moulding
of at least two women
You're a replica
You're a doll
And a doll is made to...
(laughs softly)

SHE

I'm neither young
nor old
My skin has seen better days
I already have stretch marks on my breasts
Because he gave me the skin
of a pig

HER VAGINA

A good thing too
In my case he used a different material
(*sighs with relief*)

SHE

Thanks to the correct temperature
and the humidity control
I shall remain
as I am

HER VAGINA

Dry!
Much too dry!

SHE

Wait a moment
Wait a moment
Wait a moment
A moment, wait

On a bed
of real
dead leaves,
branches and twigs
I lie on my back
with my legs open

HER VAGINA

To peep at who?
To peep at...
The fanny
The honeypot
The box
The twat
Beaver
Quim
Cunt
Pussy

SHE
In a landscape
A wooded Swiss ravine
White clouds in a blue sky
A small lake from which mist is rising
and a little waterfall
glistening in the sun

HER VAGINA
It's a photo
coloured by hand
Bits of string
Sticky tape
Transparent plastic film
Empty tins
One little motor
and one small lamp
He was a real tinkerer (I)

SHE
I lie on my back
with my legs open
And it's always an afternoon
in the late summer
when the sun occasionally disappears
behind the clouds
But the light ...
The light shines brightest on my ...
I can tell you
It isn't easy
Wait a moment
Wait a moment
Wait a moment
A moment, wait

HER VAGINA
WHEN IT'S HOT OUTSIDE
WOMEN GET HOT INSIDE

SHE
Wait a moment
Wait a moment
Wait a moment
A moment, wait
I know
A heavy silence lies over me
and over my world
Waterfall and luminous gas

balance endlessly
Time seems to have stopped

HER VAGINA
She doesn't realise
Or she pretends not to realise
But...
Dolls are imitation people
Big or small mechanical devices
you can dress
and put in a cradle
Or which you can undress
and have sex with

SHE
And I also know
that the most hypnotic thing
is my hairless cunt
so that you see its articulated forms
That gaping opening
looks like a...
vertical talking mouth

HER VAGINA
NOW I HEAR YOU TALKING BABY
LET YOUR MIND LOOSE
AND YOUR BODY WILL FOLLOW

SHE
Wait a moment
Wait a moment
Wait a moment
A moment, wait
That gaping opening
attracts the viewers' gaze
like a magnet
I suspect that it sucks in and massages
every glance
Because all those eyes
of these voyeurs
peek for hours
and always come back
again
and again

HER VAGINA
BECOME A DOLL MY DARLING
A REAL ONE

I WILL MAKE YOU
The colour of the hair,
the pubic hair and the eyes
is adjusted to suit the customer
Delivery date: at least half a year
Because there's a lot of demand
BUT FOR YOU MY DARLING
INSTANT METAMORPHOSIS
INSTANT LUCK
PERFECT MATCH

SHE
Wait a moment
Wait a moment
Wait a moment
A moment, wait
I'm in a state of repose

HER VAGINA
But I'm ready for action
I can do and say
what I like
Because no one knows what he thought...

SHE
When he made ME
he worked in secret
He said nothing about me
and he left nothing behind
There are no notes
No explanations
Plenty of questions
No answers

HER VAGINA
God created man
And the tinkerer created the doll

SHE
He worked on me
For 24 years
Underground
Alone
In silence
Until I was ready
for where I am now

HER VAGINA
Where are we?

SHE
Here!
Here we are
yet again

HER VAGINA
Yes, yet again
Entranced by illusion
That old worn-out trap
we thought we had escaped from

SHE
And where are you?
Those bachelors, where are they?
Those poor souls

HER VAGINA
I HAVE FORCED MYSELF
TO CONTRÁDICT MYSELF
IN ORDER TO AVOID CONFORMING
TO MY OWN TASTE
That was one of the tinkerer's
better songs
That's a fantastic alibi
for being open
to other tastes
I want to taste everything
on my lips

SHE
Where are you?
I can smell them
I'm here
for you...

HER VAGINA
I hope...
the people you are calling haven't forgotten
that, unlike other figures,
dolls are always there for you to violate
(*laughs*)
Subject yourself to the most passionate caresses
and to the harshest punishment
You are just a toy

SHE
The poor souls
Aren't you playing any more?
Or have I got you in my grasp?

HER VAGINA
It's an old gas lamp
you've got in your hand
And it's not exactly aflame...

SHE
Wait a moment
Wait a moment
Wait a moment
A moment, wait
Wait a moment
A moment, wait

HER VAGINA
It seems that...
you don't want it to give sufficient light
Or was that the wish
of our amateur tinkerer?

SHE
Wait a moment
Wait a moment
Wait a moment
A moment, wait
Wait a moment
Wait a moment
Wait a moment
A moment, wait
I'm no longer above you
I'm no longer a bride
I've undressed
I'm naked

HER VAGINA
GO BABY
GO AND DO IT
You want to be a female Pinocchio
You want to be a female doll
of flesh and blood

SHE
I'm no longer above you
I've come down

I'm lying on the floor...

HER VAGINA
COME DOWN
TO EARTH BABY
BE NAUGHTY
BE DARING
BUT DON'T GET CAUGHT

SHE
I lie on my back
with my legs open
on a bed of real
dead branches and twigs
waiting
Wait a moment
Wait a moment
Wait a moment
A moment, wait
Wait a moment
Wait a moment
Wait a moment
A moment, wait
It's up to you
to play the game
The game of seduction?

HER VAGINA
The game of penetration!

SHE
Or the game of art?
In which laws and possibilities
are interactive
And Eros, c'est la vie

HER VAGINA
Yet again
the same children's song
IT'S NOT THE REAL THING BABY
IT'S WISHFUL THINKING
BABY
You are a caricature
of swollen sweetness
You are a primal doll
who's gained a following
in WALT DISNEY's dream factory

SHE

The poor souls
Wait a moment
Wait a moment
A moment, wait
It's a sequel
And who knows
perhaps a conclusion too
But let the alchemy
do its work

HER VAGINA

What do you want?
You know
Women collect dolls
And men use dolls
They empty their seed into them
And who am I
to condemn that
I feel it
in the depths of my innermost being
You pretend not to hear me
because you're afraid
of hot blood
and swollen flesh

SHE

Where are you?
Where are those bachelors?
The poor souls
Come on
Come on now
Slowly but surely
Wait a moment
Wait a moment
Wait a moment
Not too fast

HER VAGINA

The best thing you can use a doll for
is to see what happens
when you drive into a wall
at 250 kilometres per hour

SHE

Wait a moment
Wait a moment
Wait a moment

A moment, wait
Wait a moment
Wait a moment
A moment, wait
I'm the queen
of the game
Powerful and dominant
like the queen
in chess

HER VAGINA
So, madam is a different sort of doll
The doll of the future perhaps?
No passive closet junkie
who lets herself be messed about
by every Tom, Dick and Harry
SHE'S A SOLDIER
A WARRIOR
A POWERGIRL
She's heavily armed
Fearless
and solitary
(*sings an extract from the Kinks' 'Lola'*)
Are you quite sure
you're a woman?

SHE
I lie on my back
with my legs open
My pose is always the same
and always right
I'm relaxed
and enjoying myself
Wait a moment
Wait a moment
Wait a moment
A moment, wait
Wait a moment
Wait a moment
Wait a moment
A moment, wait
The poor souls
Don't give up
Persevere

HER VAGINA
NO PAIN
NO GAIN

It's dogged that does it
Didn't our tinkerer say
"I want to grasp things with my mind
as the penis is grasped by the vagina"
I want to be fucked
Penetrated
Had
Banged
Tumbled
Speared
Screwed
Sprayed
Ridden
Drilled through...

I want...
I want to take
I want to grasp
I want to understand
And be understood

SHE
Wait a moment
Wait a moment
Wait a moment
A moment, wait
Wait a moment
Wait a moment
Wait a moment
A moment, wait
I'm a virgin
in full bloom
who has reached the object
of her desire
Absolute freedom
by postponing it
whatever the circumstances

HER VAGINA
Shut up
It's 5 to 10
Go back
and lie on your back
with your legs open
There's a long queue
Everyone wants to stare at you
You're immortal

SHE
Yes, they stare
because they can't do anything else
They became dolls

◆

LITTLE BODY ON THE WALL

Jan Fabre, 1996

English translation by Audrey Van Tuyckom & Gregory Ball

To Rob Scholte and Wim Vandekeybus

Sources / notes

Inspired by interviews with Orlan, Vandekeybus and other artists.

MONOLOGUE FOR A MAN

There is no woman
who knows the history of my body
better than she does
I have moved for her
walked
run
crawled
and stood still
(possibly the most difficult movement there is)
I remember as if it was yesterday
that first time
At first it irritated me
but after a few minutes I enjoyed it
I stopped moving
She stopped taking pictures
She left immediately
and said a friendly 'Have a nice day'
Nothing more
I was disappointed she'd said nothing about my body
Since then I've wanted to let my body
speak in extremes
Send it to its outermost limit
As the years went by
things reversed
When she stopped taking pictures
I stopped moving

She is an artist
Yesterday I visited her latest exhibition
A shame she wasn't there herself
I saw other eyes
go over my body
Other visitors recognized me
Not. Luckily.
At first I was a bit lost
I got lost in that hall of mirrors
Annoying!
Because I'm not the kind of person
who often stands at a mirror

I was forgetting
who I was
who she was
I tossed and turned in the museum
like a person who can't get to sleep in bed
I thought
'How should I look?'
I don't know how to look at it!

How do you look at a thing like that?
How was I to look
at my body?

I spent hours wandering
like a sprightly little ghost
that frightened itself
every time it saw its own body
before it had become a ghost
Boo boo boo
Boo boo boo
(gives himself a fright)
I looked and looked again
A wondrous trip
in an erotic machine
of burning flesh, crying bones,
risky bleeding and consuming movement
Images and more images
titillated my thoughts, memories and fantasies
about her
She who had observed my body
Or rather
had remodelled it
She had redrawn my body
by manipulating it
correcting it
modelling it
in different ways
She saw my body
as I had never looked at it before
She saw my body
as a liquid
as a vehicle
as a costume
as a trophy
as a stage
sometimes even as a battleground
But in the first place
my body was to her eyes, to her gaze
an infinite playground
divided into a number of rooms
where she found the power
to escape her limitations

I turned around and around
in a number of bodily systems
Like a person who can't wake up
in the nightmare of the day

In all the rooms
she saw my body
as a corpse
I think
'A corpse that gives cause to doubt
as to the cause of death
and that is why the law
requires an autopsy'
She was the law
While she took pictures of me
she often said
'Don't forget: every human being begins life as a woman'
And then she smiled sweetly at me
Her smile put butterflies in my belly
No, it was not a corpse
My body was a kind of dummy
Certainly in the first room
The room of the muscles
Here my body was...
a bizarre toy
whose arms, legs, feet, hands and head
can be pulled off from the torso
and the parts of this model kit
can be screwed on in other places
Muscles and tendons were no problem at all
I saw the oblique neck muscle connected
to the thigh muscle
And the biceps and the deltoid
to the anterior tibial
In other pictures
she padded me out in places
and I had an athletic figure
My muscles were contorted
and inflated like Michelin tyres
She juggled with the volume and the form
She created different shiny polished
creatures from my body
I looked like a perfect devil
a tall dwarf
a sporty satyr
a brilliant fighting machine
Full of movement
More extreme than reality
Movements and actions that laugh at death
It was as if I could overcome
the limitations of that strange
self-willed thing
that we call the body

In one large picture
I have no legs
just stumps suspended from my body
And still my body gave the impression
of possessing incredible speed
I kept on looking
and then I saw it
The rest of my body
had the lines of a race machine
I was a speed maniac
Had she given me invisible legs?
Legs that aren't there
but still feel pain
Phantom pains
Because that was what could be read from my face
Or was it the speed that was contorting my face?
Or was it pleasure?
My body had an erotic flirt
with technology
An electron tube drills a hole into my stump
through which the prosthesis sucks my stump in
An embrace of superfluous flesh and plastic fibres
Everything she knew about me
or everything that had been said between us
she used and misused
At that moment I realized
that I had once told her about a friend
who had lost both his legs
in a car accident
And that I thought it was terrible for him
Then she reacted with a strange look
and a remarkable reply
She said
'You mustn't be sentimental
You should consider an accident
as a life-force
If you were to lose your legs
you could move even more beautifully for me'
I failed to understand her then
And now after seeing her work
I know what she wanted to say
But I don't want to understand her
It's as if she wants to kill everything physical between us
with her thoughts

I was reminded of the day I'd hurt myself
on bits of broken glass that fell from above
in a performance by another artist

with monkey tricks
(Yes, yes, it happens,
sometimes monkeys drop bits of broken glass from above)
And then you get clumsy little ghosts
who go and stand underneath them
like me
The white shards pierced my flesh
and scratched against the joints
and the bones of my skeleton
My body was full of gaping wounds
I was covered in blood and bits of my bowels
were hanging out of my body
Bowels stuck all over with
little white slivers that reflected the light
I looked like a congealed whirlwind
I was sick of pain
And it was precisely that day
she wanted to take pictures of me
She was sweet
and tried to cheer me up
She has a strange sense of humour
and she said
'Time heals everything!
And what's more...
A body without scars or mutilations
has no beauty for me'

So I let her take pictures of me
While I moved for her
I started to feel more and more
like a shaman of the olden days
My body starting talking, getting louder
and more and more energetic
I think I must have been in a kind of trance
A visible ecstasy of pain
which she probably enjoyed
After she'd observed me for a long time
with that typical look of hers
she emerged from behind her lenses
and said, whispering
'I see you're enjoying the fact that I'm taking pictures of you'
I was shy
and blushed a little
I replied
'It excites me
It gives me a kick'
On her face I saw a smile of confusion
I reacted at once and said

'No, no, not sexually
I feel my body better
when others look at me
I have the feeling that I am more real then
that I live more, exist more
I experience every point in the movements I make
as new
Every part of a movement is an event
a happening
a spectacle
It is as if I've been dead
and come to life again
Do you understand me, a little?'
She didn't reply
and smiled in a friendly way
I thought she understood me
and then she said
'You don't have a head for business
and I like that
But you have a body for pleasure
and I can do business with that'
At that moment I didn't understand
what she meant by that
Now I do of course

Because in room two
The room of the digestive system
I saw close-up pictures
of bloody
slimy
and sticky guts
cut out of my body
Bits of flesh, at very low prices
because the instruments of the plastic surgeons
and the biotechnologists were still in them
On other pictures in the same room
my organs are blown up
to superhuman proportions
My stomach is my torso
My gullet and liver are my arms
my pancreas and gall-bladder are my legs
my large and small intestines are my feet and hands
The rectum is one big bloody eye
A glassy body
consisting of a gelatinous substance
that seems to talk
The anus is my mouth that can see
and through which I shit my own flesh

and eat it up again
I was reminded of
that look in her eyes
That hungry look
that wants to devour everything
She often said
'The lens is not a mirror
Don't look into the lens!
And if you want to admire yourself
you'd better look with your anus
Because the anus is the face
of the only religion I believe in'
So she was allowed to admire my behind
In dozens of small pictures
hung randomly
I am half organ and half machine
sweating blood
pissing tears
and vomiting shit
A human power machine that explodes
by its daily mutation,
hormone preparations
and face-lifted reality
The torn limbs
are flying about
like angry bullets
biting hammers
and burning knives of chrome
Weapons wrapped in magnetic foil
to prevent my flesh from rotting
PLAY
FAST FORWARD
AND REWIND
so that my body
melts back together again
into a robot
who is human

In room three
The room of the cardiovascular system
I saw images of my body
which appeared
and disappeared
Feverish figures
gaunt and starved creatures
who seemed like ghostly apparitions
In these pictures, my skin
is very vulnerable and light-grey

as thin as cigarette paper
I saw movement
that wasn't there
I saw blood
coursing through my arteries and veins
Small trickles kept converging
into larger streams of blood
My body weighed nothing
and seemed liquid
In the hollow of my skinny body
I saw the aorta
comfort a lump of flesh
that was no longer beating
but shivering
with horror and privation
Was I on a diet?
Was my body that haggard?
Had I trained that hard?
In one black-and-white photograph
a stomach torn open
under the weight of human flesh
Was I a cannibal?
Had I tortured myself so?
Had I worn out my body so?
Dreams and nightmares
from earlier times
were manipulated by her images
and told to me again
Was I seeing my own body
or the body of my grandfather
on his return from the concentration camp
Because of all these memories
I started to get nervous
I got anxious
got dizzy, and passed out
and up

I knew that I had arrived in room four
The room of the nervous system
I didn't want to look
but I looked like people look at an accident
Very quickly and filled with sensation
I saw pictures
I think
of my body
consisting of a little heap
of cells and tissues at war with each other
I started sweating

I couldn't watch
my nervous links and fibres
Those allegedly perfect information channels
which at that moment were giving the wrong
impulses and stimuli to my head
and to the juice in my backbone
It was as if I was putting my hand on a hot stove
and there was no quick protective movement
of spontaneous withdrawal
My organ of fear
started beating faster
It thumped and thumped
I could no longer count the beats
Of course I recognized the symptoms
A stinging in my eyes
pinpricks in my cheeks
a pressure on my chest
a tingling in my hands and feet
a dry mouth
And the feeling that my head
was getting too much blood and not enough oxygen
I thought I was suffocating
I was floating
for the umpteenth time
between life and death
Boo boo boo
Boo boo boo
Carefully
full of tenderness
tact and shrewdness
I talked to
my organ of fear
and befriended it
I started to breathe
more slowly and consciously
Breathing in through my nose
And breathing out through my mouth
Slowly I came down
and knew where I was again
For the 111th time
I had sent death on leave

And oh irony
I found myself in room five
The room of the respiratory system
On silvery pictures
in a red velvet frame
my torso is chopped into innumerable

little pieces
and hung on meat hooks
The anonymous meat
is well-smoked
My lungs are ashtrays
My larynx and trachea
are ablaze
From the cavity of my nose
comes red smoke
And in the cavity of my mouth there's a graveyard
where two healthy sharp canines stick up
It reminded me
of that one moment
when, with that piercing look of hers
she observed me for a long time
Then she sharpened her teeth
with the tip of her tongue
and smiled
And then I thought
'Now she will bite my neck
and suck the blood from my body'
But nothing of the kind
She said
'Slurp some more cancer sticks
The smoke looks good on the photos
It gives your skin a lived-in shine
And then your body radiates a desire
to be investigated at close quarters'
I'd been wanting to smoke the whole time
But yes,
that's what you get in those damned museums
There's no real life
Only the forbidden and the imaginary
I looked around me
and at that moment I saw no other visitors
I listened
and heard only the wheeze of my breathing
It asked for more
I lit a cigarette
blew a tiny little ghost from my mouth
and sauntered on
To the next room

Room six
The room of the urinary passages
It was more like a display case
On the walls to the left and right there were
small photographs of my kidneys

They looked like working and fucking ants
collecting my urine
drinking it and pissing it out again
It was absurd and cruel
On the middle wall
one small picture
of my bladder about to burst
I nearly wet my pants
laughing
It reminded me of
that time I had given everything
what was in my body
I was soaking with sweat
and I needed a pee
and she said
'How's that? I haven't stopped taking pictures yet
Let it go
I want to see all your bodily fluids'
I started spitting at her
She didn't find that funny
Until I let everything go
It was a warm and pleasant feeling
And then I saw in her eyes
that she was enjoying me
And I said
'Isn't it glorious
to be able to forget
who you are or what you're doing
That the intensity of the moment
gives you no other choice
and other things decide in your place
It's like falling in love
Isn't it that you surrender your own safety?
That ecstasy gets a chance?'
She looked me up and down
and replied very calmly
'I always know perfectly what I'm doing
But if I am a monkey in your eyes
you mustn't first cut me open
and then say: Damn, that monkey is dead
It's an illusion to think
that you can analyse me
and that you understand what's on my mind'

In room seven
The room of the lymphatic system
I saw
my body

wholly transparent
A heavenly body
with the stars in the wrong places
The lymph nodes of the groin, the belly,
the armpits and the neck
have moved to the toes and fingers
so that they
are doing serious harm to my body
They are turning the entire immune system
upside down
in a manner of speaking
On large luminous colour photographs
I crawl into all the holes in my body
My hands disappear into my arse
and my feet are devoured by my mouth
It reminded me of my youth
And of my father who was a vet
I often had to help him
With my little arms
I could penetrate better
into cows' behinds
to pull the calves out
when the delivery was going wrong
Sometimes I crawled inside up to my knees
And then I thought, proudly
'I live in a body
that is larger than mine' *(laughs)*

She found variations and diseases
for every part of my body
She saw my body as the intruder
in my own body
An enemy
A dangerous germ
A magic globe of a cancer cell
A monkey that's ill
and passes on infection
She saw my body
as an unstoppable monstrous virus
that devours all organs
and leaves itself behind
as a pale shell
So I was her dear little... *(laughs)*
ghost
Boo boo boo
Boo boo boo
Every shame that existed
she gave my body

Naturally there were images
of my decaying flesh
Did she want to tell me
that every desire to touch
at the same time creates a distance?
Or did she want to tell me
that you can't touch!
Is the warmth of touch a danger to her?
My body was aching
for the power of pride
I thought
'Is that what she wants?'
Or did she want my body
to have only the strength of an addiction?
Addicted to her look
'Yes, yes,' I thought
'I am getting to know her a little'
and I imagined her saying:
'Without my look, your body
again becomes the body it always was
A snare of loneliness and misunderstanding'
She started haunting my head
I no longer knew what I was seeing
I no longer knew what I was saying
I heard her voice in my head
singing a refrain
'Little body on the wall
Who has the most beautiful blood corpuscles of them all?
Little body on the wall
Who has the most beautiful blood corpuscles of them all?'

In the next room
Room eight
The room of the skeleton
I saw my body
cut open and ripped apart in different ways
My bones and cartilage were rearranged
in crazy ways
I changed into all kinds of
small animals and enormous insects
which can hinge and bend
every which way
I could dig, turn, chop,
drill, bore, and stamp
fine and coarse
I thought
'Although I have a feeling for animals
I don't think you should humanize them

as so many do these days'
I started remembering things
I thought I had forgotten
When I was a boy of about eleven
I was bitten by a dog
I felt that pain
again
I looked at my scar
and saw my arm swollen and ripped open
I didn't cry
It was as if the world stood still
Me here, the world there
and between us, one great stream of blood
I though it was exciting
to look at that open wound
and see the imprint of the dog's teeth
in my radius and ulna
Until my father, in a panic,
disturbed my discovery
and tied up my arm below the shoulder
But he was too late
The dog's saliva
had found its way to my heart
And since then I've had rabies
Woof woof woof
Woof woof woof
(barks like a caged rabid dog)

The body consists of eleven systems
with interlocking functions
These systems are the same in men and women
Except (laughs)
Except for
the hormonal system and the reproductive system
Rooms nine and ten
I saw a foetus
containing an egg-cell and a sperm cell
with my features
Like fully-grown astronauts
with a golden skin
they float around and keep on changing
their sex and age
My glands hang outside my body
They mutate quickly
They are bulges and lumps which seem to regulate
new functions
At that moment I was reminded
of the time I was ill

and didn't want to be photographed
She was angry
and looked at me for a long time
with a piercing look
A look that tried to suck my soul from my body
And then she said in a serious tone
'If you want to, you can change
the relation between yourself and the world
If you dare to use all the means at your disposal
then you won't get ill anymore'
I didn't answer
but thought
'What means?'
If you want to take pictures of a ghost,
go ahead'
I went to lie down in my bed
and didn't get up again
I regularly misbehaved during those hours
like a child
Boo boo boo
Boo boo boo
Until she got nervous
and almost wanted to hit me
I said 'Do me a favour
any change would be welcome'
She smiled
and answered calmly
'You shouldn't teach
an old monkey new tricks
I will help you to change'
Now I know what she meant *(smiles)*
In beautiful colour photographs
she hung Fallopian tubes, ovaries and a womb in my mouth
In my right eye socket a vas deferens and prostate
In my left eye socket, testicles
I was born
from my new mask
like a beautiful snake-like hermaphrodite
like a black crippled Nureyev
and like a young woman who looks old
She gave me overfull pendulous breasts
and a sagging wrinkled belly
And still my body stayed beautiful
The smile that seems to vibrate throughout my entire body
reveals that I am aware
of the fear my flesh inspires
I looked like a saint
And then I saw

I had become her Mary
depicted in strange and different ways
I thought
'Do I really exist for her
or just in her imagination?'
Mary is made up only of ideas
'And me?
Do I exist?' I asked myself
Yes, I exist by the grace of her pictures
her images and impressions of me
In black-and-white photos, I saw that she gave
my body the glory of her way of moving
How she moved with refinement, elegance and subtlety
when she took pictures of me
In every picture my bodily tears
were visible
Were they my tears
or her sweat?
I had the feeling that she had crawled
under my skin

Maybe that's why the last room was
Room eleven
The room of the skin
I saw that
my sensitive protective layer
took on strange forms
Certain bones tore open
my natural shell
They are deliberate incisions
made from the inside
in decoration
Around other parts of my body
a metal carapace
is stretched taut like the hide on a drum
On large colour slides I saw that my body sheds its skin
like reptiles do
My skin changes into all the colours of the rainbow
My nails are spikes
and my hair is made of steel wires
growing in and over each other over my body
Because the skin from the soles of the feet
and the palms of the hand
was grafted onto the rest of my body
I looked like an imperishable organ
that rejects everything
I asked myself
'What is this woman looking for?

For what?
For whom?'
I became a little sad
and thought
'I would lick your body wet like an animal
I would dry your body with the kisses of a human being'
But I was immediately reminded
of that time
when I once said to her
'I find you attractive
You have a skin that invites
the touch'
She looked at me
with seductive eyes
and smiled in excitement
I thought
But she replied
'I know you
I'm always looking at you
I observe your body
You let your picture be taken
But you don't know me!
You'd better not touch my skin
My skin is treacherous
I have the skin of an angel, but I'm a vulture
I have the skin of a woman, but I'm a man
I have the skin of a live being, but I'm a dead soul
in search of another body
Because I've left my body
and can't find it anymore'

Looking back now
and having visited her exhibition
I know it wasn't a seductive look I saw
Her eyes always had that same look
A predatory look
Well, I can't describe it any other way
It wasn't a look
that wanted to encompass me
It wasn't a look
that wanted to fuse with mine
like I have seen in other women
Her look wanted to isolate me from the world
so that she could do everything
with me she wanted to
I have always felt alone with her
lonely and separated from the rest of the world
I believe in the fear some people feel

of having their picture taken
They are afraid the picture
will take away their soul
I feel robbed of something
although I don't know precisely what
Sometimes her images killed something in me
But with their help
I restored myself to life
The people who visit her exhibition
think we have a relationship
or used to have a relationship
All those strange eyes
reading the story of my body
which makes them think they know me
They know nothing
Moving or dancing
that's my nature
Change is my essence
A continual becoming
I'm always on my way to the other
I am always yearning for...
For fusion with the things
around me
If that's not possible
I want at least to fuse
with the person I care about
But in all those years
that she took pictures of me
she never touched me
Not once

◆

THE EMPEROR OF LOSS

Jan Fabre, 1994-2005

English translation by Gregory Ball

© Wonge Bergmann, 2005

For Tommy Cooper

Sources / notes

Inspired by the work of Tommy Cooper and Arthur Rimbaud.

(1) The answer given by the American General Mc. Auliffe to the German request
for an 'honourable surrender' of Bastogne
(2) Obladi Oblada, The Beatles, Lennon & McCartney
(3) When I'm 64, The Beatles, Lennon & McCartney
(4) After Zhuang Zi, Taoist philosopher
(5) Sympathy for the Devil, The Rolling Stones, Jagger & Richards
(6) Jean de Boisson
(7) Zorba the Greek, Nikos Kazantzakis
(8) Maria, West Side Story, Leonard Bernstein and Stephen Sondheim
(9) Romeo and Juliet, Act 2, scene 2, William Shakespeare
(10) Paul Van Ostayen
(11) My way, Paul Anka and Frank Sinatra
(12) Joseph Beuys
(13) Andy Warhol
(14) Jean Baudrillard

MONOLOGUE FOR A MAN

It has already beaten 1 billion times
pumped 125 million litres
And sometimes it feels like it has
already beaten 2 billion times
and pumped 250 million litres
Am I old?
Or am I young?
Can I do anything?
Do I know anything?
Do I know the secret of changing life?
Do I know the secret of improving the world?
Do I know the secret
of dreaming the unsolvable dream?
I want to be always old and young
Am I the first human
who can live without a living heart?
Do I have an artificial heart?
Or do I have a heart for... *(laughs)*
Is this comic
or is it cosmic?
I have navigated every storm of suffering
I have experienced every form of erring
Longed to play chess with mirrors
I have danced over smoke and clouds
Known love between trees and sand
Almost drunk the Scheldt dry
Shakespeare has acted with me
I have cried together with apes
Directed diabolical traffic with swords
Stolen the poison from all the rats
and given boredom richness
And I want
I want
I want to begin
I want to begin again
False start
Watch my words
The end won't work either
I want to begin again
And make you laugh
I'm a beginner
I want to forget everything
I'm beginning again
But... but the refusal
I have never forgotten
I never want to forget
Nor unlearn
The not wanting to

The daring to say 'no'
Njet
Nuts [1]
Not surrendering
The refusal
By refusing
I have as it were
on a few square centimetres
conjured up
whole lives and worlds
Parties in the night
Nothing went wrong
but everything got out of hand
A poet-magician was I
But was I a farmer too?
A farmer
who had to work in the field
of reality
Let's slog
we all slog
together
What solidarity
Let's get going
What an eternal gratitude
Anchors up and down countless times
Chains grew invisibly tight and loose
Mirrors without lead were made
The rats never ceased
and took on everything
Even the cleaning of unsullied windows
A sadness
overcame me
And I tripped over long toes
Apparently I was funny
They laughed at me, didn't they?
I didn't understand any of it
of the magician I was
It turned out I could do 'something'
Sometimes I could
make 'something' appear
and disappear
And I also had a body
I could imitate insects with.
I could even act a little.
(imitates insects and people)

It doesn't work
anymore like it used to

That's why I'm practising
And you know practice makes perfect *(laughs ironically)*

I was musical
I had a good voice too
and had a feeling for spectacle
And that was what people wanted
They don't want revolution
They want spectacle disguised
as revolution
the revolution of the laugh
of the magician I was
Had I lied to myself so much?
What else could I do?
I have already done everything
Fortunately
the lying
I never want to forget
I never have forgotten
never unlearned
Like the refusal
At the right time
a lie for the best
is never wrong
I have to fool myself completely
into actually doing it
Although I like doing it
Nothing, that's what I like doing most
The flight into nothing
even when it doesn't work
I'm the emperor of loss
and am Lancelot who rapes
princesses in the night
In my imagination
I have to do something
So I practise doing nothing
I want to dream the unsolvable dream
Look I'm practising
Practice makes perfect *(laughs)*

Oh, I'm losing my balance
It's never happened before
I'm still looking for my balance
Does my body have the right weight?
Does my body have the right balance?
You can laugh
I carry it in a pouch now
not in my body

but in my hand
Yes, I know
It sounds strange
but it's true
It was in a pouch in my body too
The problem was, it pumped and pumped so hard
that it became too big for the pouch in my body
The pouch turned into armour that stopped
the internal fire and the expansion of heat
It could no longer pump so well
It lives in another pouch now
IF THERE ARE NO PROBLEMS
THERE ARE NO SOLUTIONS
Another problem is, I have lived nowhere else
Others have lived in my head
Obladi oblada
Obladi oblada
Life goes on [2]
New ones came
others went
some stayed
Roses are red
Violets are blue
Sugar is sweet and so are you
Will you still need me
Will you still feed me
When I'm 64 [3]
I'm always on the road
and live in the things I do
or dream

Have you seen it?
It's a disguised mirror
It is
doing nothing
With nothing in my hands
with nothing up my sleeve
nothing in my pockets
That is the power of clowns' dreams
and of making people laugh
as if they were going to sleep
with other ideas
It's that small mirror
that I keep in the most pleasant places

I see
It sounds strange to your ears
But that's not the way I want to hear

I refuse to

I was asleep
In a deep glow
Unable to be woken
In full flight
I was panting
in my realm of shadows
I wanted to dream the unsolvable dream
Surmise the supreme pleasure
Sometimes you have to be wide awake
to see the sense of nonsense
To distinguish the useless
and never to reach the useful
The pleasure of life deceived
Like Fairy Footsteps behind the back
who I see isn't so mad
who I see hasn't yet been seen
Are your mirrors dull?
Everyone knows the use
of the useful
but no one knows the consumption
of the useless [4]
You can laugh even more at the useless

You hadn't seen it?
Otherwise you would have laughed
I hope there'll still be laughter tonight

I know, hope is false
but gives life;
survive and eat whatever can't fly
Isn't it any good?
Then I'll begin again
I want to begin again
I want to begin
I'm like that
At any moment
I can begin again
I begin again
and again
It's hard
but I begin
I begin
again
I'll forget everything
but the refusal
I wish never to forget

I have never forgotten
never unlearned
I laid this pouch on the scales
and as a counterweight
a feather
on the other side
Will it ever balance?
Yes, it will balance one day
I knew it
that you wouldn't laugh
I know the feeling
of failure
of loss
I've known those serious mugs
all my life
those customary bastards
always with that bullshit
about (being right or wrong)

Always stay polite
Excuse me
It's not to you
I said it to myself
No, I said it to this ant
This one, in front of me, shouted
What are you standing here for?
Listen, sometimes it works
Sometimes it doesn't
It usually doesn't
like flying
So, why am I standing here?
But I try
I try again and again
I keep on trying from time to time
Perhaps to see the anchors of our longing
together
Perhaps the real reason is: vanity
A sort of fettered longing
to belong after all
Do you hear that?
I refuse to hear
the way you hear!
I refuse
I refuse to understand
I'm not so easy to hire
And am seldom or never asked
I'm too dangerous
No one can take me for a ride

No one can direct me
There are exceptions, of course
Cut off like me
But even that one idiot
can't tell me everything
Maybe there's my gallows
All alone in the world
but with a dream

There was once a double idiot
with clownish tricks
who allowed the 8-hour dada-blabla
daily activities of animals
and people to triumph
It was as people said
and still say now
and usually encounter
in tents like this:
'This is theatre like it was to be expected and foreseen'
Sometimes in the evening
Sometimes from night to morning
getting dressed and undressed
and dressed and undressed
Washing, eating, drinking
sitting, shitting, standing, smoking
It was nothing but work, work, work
I blew till I saw stars

I'm longing
to make it work
or to sometimes make something work
I want to discover
So I have invited
myself
I can't do without
I want the supreme pleasure
In which position
shall I carry the pouch?
In my belly
or on my belly?
I want to know its lightness
I won't refuse
I need it
To practise
Practice makes perfect *(laughs)*

That's why I'm standing here
Perhaps the nature of the creature?

Where's that ant?
It doesn't give up
You can swat it
stamp on it or crush it
It doesn't give up
Perhaps it's the creature's assertiveness?
So what sort of monster am I?
An earthworm?
A fly for one day?
Or am I that ant?
I keep on trying
and keep on trying again
I keep on trying and am capable
of standing up to anything
I keep on trying to reduce
my lack of true pride
And above all I want to dream the unsolvable dream
It is also the ultimate pleasure
of trying
See how I leave this new invention
–I mean the idea as an invention–
unsabotaged
You're wondering why?
It will satisfy you this time
So many expectant mothers
fell on their belly
Perhaps that's why I practise?
And practice makes perfect *(laughs)*

Did you like it?
Wasn't it enthralling?
Did it fail again?
There was a fleet
that sailed to Spain
when it returned
it came again
The child inside me isn't dead yet
I haven't yet lost
the anchors of longing
The buoys are still floating
in my shit
Anyone standing here still has hope
Even that ant
Even this child
that laughs and makes you laugh

The big child, that I am
The big thief, that I am

The ant crawls among the maggots
The ant that is guilty of a series of deeds
too horrible to describe here
But I can't do anything about it
Sometimes it's Jekyll and Hyde
A preparation for later
when I become the unsolvable dream?
It almost happened to me once
A hallucinatory flight became a hangover
I made a mistake once
The rats laughed at me
and didn't run off
I simply like human flesh
And at dusk
I was the dealer
in 99%-pure mirror snow
for beautiful children
from 7 to 77 years old
I want the perfection
The supreme pleasure
The sublime pleasure
I want to be a murderer today too
Tonight I want to be Fred Astaire
Without standing on tiptoe
without a raised head
without raising my arms
everything will indicate
that the upward movement
is present
without wanting to prove
that a one-man counter-movement
is possible
I feel it
It will happen
WITH YOUR HEART IN THE RIGHT PLACE
YOU DON'T WRITE HISTORY
It would explain why you
belong with certain people
Even with people whom you have never seen before
and with whom you immediately feel an affinity

Shall I carry my heart on my head?
Or shall I eat my heart?
Where do I begin?
Because like everything
it consists of two parts
Which would be the tastiest part?
The left side or the right side

Left and right are separated completely
by a partition
Or is it a mirror?
The left half and the right half again both consist
of two chambers
In which chamber am I now?
I'll just begin again
I can always
begin again
with the real illusion
It's the first time
I begin
and again
and again
I'm looking for
Perhaps... recognition
Do I exist?
Am I disguised as a mirror?
Or am I a dwarf
or an ape?
A deed or a dream?
A murder or a suicide?
What am I?
Perhaps that's why I'm practising?
And practice makes perfect

But apparently
I do not yet
exist
by the grace
of a lack
Laughter?
Recognition?
Appreciation?
Yes, that's what I want
A pat on the back once in a while?
You don't have to knock me senseless
A bit of applause once in a while?
Not till I die, of course
A little attention once in a while?
You don't have to suffocate me
And you don't have to swallow everything
I do
or say
Isn't that friendly?
Here is the ant
That modest servant of beauty
of laughter

Please allow me to introduce myself
I'm a man of wealth and taste
I've been around for many long years
Stole many men's soul and fame
I was around when Jesus Christ
Had his moments of doubt and pain
Made damn sure that Pilate
Washed his hands and sealed his fate

Pleased to meet you
Hope you guess my name
But what's puzzlin' you
Is just the nature of my game (5)
...

Perhaps this ant is
a dictator
or a plush ape
or a plush rabbit
or a devilish clown
A devilish clown
who's afraid of his own fire
Who wants to dream the unsolvable dream
Wants to imagine the supreme pleasure
The possibility of failure
makes only greater
my longing
for something to work sometimes
That's why I'm practising
And practice makes perfect

Wasn't it any good again?
I thought it was a great success
I do want a bit of appreciation
A little bit
A very little bit
Because I'm here
No?
For the ant then?
A very little bit?
A very very little bit?
piccolo
piccolo
or do I have to be a gigolo?
That's no problem
I can be almost everything
only not what I want to be

But I suspect that I can

But I'm not going to say
whose gigolo I am
So you'd like to know that?
I might have known
That typical vulgar curiosity
I really hadn't expected any different
Wanting to gossip about private affairs
Shall I reveal a few in passing?
It will then be told and passed on
blown up and increased tenfold
by the press and media
In order to address
the so-called public that
couldn't be here tonight
and to give them a thin reply
That public that no longer takes the time
to discover the value of pain
That public that no longer has the time
to read
to watch
to listen
or to laugh
and wants only chatter
The clown would never chatter
and his conscience would only share the knowledge
Even in his devilish language

In which position should I carry my heart?
Which part of my heart shall I eat?
I admire no one
who gives me no excesses
and who himself has known no extreme life
I admire the renegade
in myself
who hopes to fall back upward
And who wants to dream the unsolvable dream
Wants to imagine the supreme pleasure
Wants to feel the sublime pleasure
Row upon row
Shoulder to shoulder
you are sitting
Strange?
Strangeness and cruelty strike
in unexpected places
Places of delusion?
Places of kinship?

I don't admire
you
Although, at least you are still here
to be a witness
To what?
To my dream?
To my sadness?
Or my failure?
Or is your presence
a form of appreciation?
Of whom?
Of that insect, of that ant?
Is it still standing here?
Yes, yes, on its hind legs
Now say 'thank you '

POPOV
I appreciate him
POPOV
he could turn lead into gold
and tears into laughter
He appreciated the audience
I mean, the audience appreciated him
But the problem is...
The name Popov
represents 'authority' to the audience
The authority of laughter
Don't forget
It's not PAVLOV, but POPOV
Around our pillows golden ladders rise
And up and down the skies
With wingéd sandals shod
The angels come and go
Appreciation from many people...
Such a reward would be a punishment
I would refuse that honour
The refusal as a lifebuoy
of penance
or as an anchor
for guilt broken loose
People more often laugh from cowardice
than because they are amused
One laughs more often out of cowardice
than because one is amused [6]

If Popov
has had 100 people
who have watched

listened
and laughed well
for the right reasons
then he can count himself lucky
He can kiss his hands
lick his fingers
or laugh himself dead in his grave
It would do him good
It would cheer him up
Since he was very sad
I've never known anyone so sad
He said : 'My audience is too large
and so I have no one anymore'
Who am I talking to now?
Is that ant still here?
Yes, it's here
I'm talking to no one
I'm talking to myself
I create the other
for whom I long
Am I looking at you?
Or are you looking at me?
Or are you looking at each other?
Are we in a hall of mirrors here?
Where am I now?
Did I eat the left chamber
or the left front chamber?
Or was it the right chamber
and the right front chamber
I ate?
Always these damned reflections
Can't we compete?
Always these contradictions
Can't we draw any conclusions from them?
Don't we want to communicate?
Those mirrors everywhere and always
Everywhere we see ourselves
Everywhere I see myself
Everywhere that look of enquiry
Everywhere that look of hope
for an answer
for recognition
It's as if someone were following me
knowing that I'm going nowhere
A shadow as a cancerous growth?
Or is it the spell that surrounds me
The echo of laughter
or the echo of a new beginning

I want to begin
I want to begin again
I'm a beginner
It is difficult
But I don't want to remember anything
of what I've said or done
I can begin again at any time
I begin again
Forget everything
except the refusal
I've never forgotten that
I never want to forget it
never unlearn
I need something
to survive
to live
Is it possible
to be steady
To fight against yourself
your whole life
and so against others
that you don't want to meet
that you don't want to know
Or rather turn
along with the weathercock
in the circus of belief
in mediocrity
The power of the compromise
The theatre of the cultivated
madness
You notice no difference between
what is necessity
what is pretence
Is it the reflection?
Left becomes right
right becomes left
The pretence becomes a necessity
and vice versa
Have we all
become emperors without clothes
dancing a tango with each other
to Wagners' Funeral March?
Can you accept this?

The tailor makes the man
WHEN THERE'S NO MYTH
THERE'S NO MAN
That double idiot with his clownish tricks

I spoke about earlier
Together we demolished and tore apart
life as theatre
I ran until I saw the powerlessness
I danced myself unconscious
EVERY MAN NEEDS A LITTLE BIT
OF MADNESS [7]
I was rising
but still I kept on falling
Breathing became panting
Panting became silence
and remaining faithful
to the idea of transcending
The obscure body of the night
The weightless body in power

Where is that ant?
That wants to dream the unsolvable dream
That wants to imagine the supreme pleasure
Wants to feel the sublime pleasure
Will I no longer know the duality
that characterizes our lives?
Do I want to stand forever with feet together?
And sing the delusions?
Is that why I practise?
Does practice make perfect?

(sings)
Maria
The most beautiful sound I ever heard
Maria, Maria, Maria, Maria...
All the beautiful sounds of the world in a single word
Maria, Maria, Maria, Maria...
I just met a girl named Maria
And suddenly the name will never be the same to me [8]
...

What's in a name? [9]
Popov, no Pavlov
Always those images
to which we react
in which we recognize ourselves
or rather don't recognize ourselves
Distorted mirrors
Ghostly mirrors
like the memory
Sometimes images
too far to see

Sometimes images
that are here and now
The more mistakes
and failures I have
in my practising
the better I can look into the future
that was
and always returns
I will experience a changed time
Here time is a line of gentle fire
of which we only experience
the blue of the low flame 'now'
There it's possible to survey the whole line
of all the colours in the blazing fire
So that I can know the pleasure
of a female pyromaniac
Who's burning there?
What's burning there?
Who has that madness?
Who has that fever?
Who's that silent one?
That silence that wails and roars
I'm here!
Who saves his words
and burns his money
and lets his stone parrot screech
I'm here!
I'm here!
Who's that running along with his suit full of money
Who's that running along with his clown's face
and runs
and runs
and runs
against the wall
of the Ankerrui
This is no theatre
His face in shreds
and the wall coloured red
It's a filled dock
In the most remote places
he's standing shouting and raging
I'm here!
I'm here!
I'm here!
Who's that there whispering
his balls off
Who's that there screaming
in the bastion

of the rats of the air
Who's there amongst the gulls
on the roof of the Central Station
during the rush-hour of the night
covered in shit during a full moon
No one hears him
No one understands him
Who is that clown?
that whispers to his
mirror image
Give me the look
on the other side
Give me the feeling
of both sides
I'm that clown
I'm the malcontent with wings
I'm the rebel who doesn't fall
I'm the resistance fighter who flies
I'm the dreamer who transcends everything
In the flight of the void
In the flight of powerlessness

I'm the emperor of loss
Yes go on, laugh
I thank you
I want to be that chosen one
If I get the time
to practise enough
Because practice makes perfect

I'm that star, that insect in the night
I'm the earthworm that's trampled on
and always comes back and begins again
Where is that ant?
Here's that ant
Shall I wear my heart on my heals?
One left chamber for my right foot
and one right chamber for my left foot?
One day it will become clear who I am
I want to raise myself infinitely high
above the clouds, feel myself
and seek what lies behind it
Perhaps
The discovery of the pleasure
that only the other knows?
Pride will from now on
no longer be punished
The sense of guilt will be taunted

until laughter breaks out
No, you shouldn't laugh now
If you want to laugh, go ahead...
That's what I'm practising for
and practice makes perfect *(laughs)*

Thank you
I saw and see everywhere
here too
my seriousness is laughed at
Therefore
again and again
the refusal
in my head
In this impenetrable joke
oracles are sitting grinning
apparently always waiting
to be laughed at
I always was a ridiculous child
When I wanted to make people cry
only then did they laugh
Why?
Who are those people
who have no memory or recollection
who never want to begin again
who are everywhere and always
and want to give their own substance to life

In the accursed school
of imposed time that punishes and envies
where tears dance for fear
and trees give no oxygen
In that maze I wander around
Like a hermit of the night
that likes to hear laughter
I'm seeking
and doubts seek me
And I begin again
And I seek
and doubts seek me
I don't want to accept
everything just like that
Sometimes only rather lesser deeds
And not to sit waiting, yearning
for the evening and the night
Why the refusal of the day?
Because I once stepped on it as a child
and was ill for weeks afterwards

from that 8-hour complaint
The worst thing is...
that complaint is general and meanly arranged
For every Tom, Dick and Harry
Hello there
are you still here?
And where's that ant?
This was, 'Tom says good morning to everything' [10]
He would have been better off oversleeping
Said the doctor to the patient
Am I really a clown?
Or am I the doctor on duty?
Which monster are they talking about
when they're talking about me
–can you get
a bigger version of me too?–
About a little ant?
Yes, it is still here
About a dayfly
About a catastrophe with wings
About a mirror that doesn't fall
About a gangster who flies
About a dreamer who transcends everything
Was it an ultrasound of the future
or an echo of the past?
They really let me know
because the doctors possess all that chatter
The patient, the pupil
I alone
with my conscience and knowing
what I wanted to share
What I have done?
Nothing, only refused

The rats were laughing themselves to death
They rolled and twirled, leaped in the air
I shouldn't have robbed them
What I stole saved their lives
I was tested
I was crammed full
with another sort of poison
I was compelled to swallow repose
That's why, again and again
The refusal
I was...
What is madness?
Madness, too much reality?
Madness, the absolute refusal?

Or is madness
wanting to dream the unsolvable dream?
The sheet of white paper
was to me a vital kidney
And yet I had to
with or without pleasure
A tree
It had to be a tree
and someone of the opposite sex
Why?
The madness of the demand
and of the therefore
I tore their mirroring
masks off
and crushed them
With the splinters I carved
into my being
I didn't draw a tree
I became a tree
My skin became the bark
The leaves rustled
on my arms, which were branches
My feet became roots
that clung tightly to the cold ground
to endure the hurricane of pleasure
Under my tree which supplied oxygen
I became Adam and Eve
They became afraid
Afraid of what?
Afraid of my rustling that was a storm
Afraid of my penis that I pressed
between my female breasts
Afraid of the hissing of the snake I had become
Afraid of the bellowing of the ape I saw
I was the creation
I lived
I created that
from which they can never be born
I recognized a tremor of pleasure in their bodies
Tortures that laugh
in their horrible silence
Tortures that shit
in their misplaced speech
Cockroaches
that shat
Shit in their heads
on the walls and on the floor
And I ate it up

It was so moreish
I can, always and everywhere,
begin again
and again
and again
as a beginner
with the realistic illusion
It is the first time
I'm beginning
again
I can forget everything
except the refusal
I have never forgotten that
I never want to forget it
never unlearn
They became even more afraid
Of what?
Of the reflections
of their broken masks
They saw themselves crying
with delight
The civilized apes
More afraid than afraid
they were
Of what?
Of the madness of the unsolvable dream
they never dare dream
The supreme pleasure they never dare imagine
Because enjoyment is dangerous
I was no longer allowed to draw
I was no longer allowed to move
Was I tested and crammed full
before I knew it?
Before I knew it
I stood still
and lay immobile
Vertical became horizontal
horizontal became oval
Male internal Psychiatry: MIP
Female internal Psychiatry: FIP
MIP and FIP
2 buoys
FIP and MIP
or was it 2 anchors?
MIP and FIP
Left became right
and right became under and above
FIP and MIP

MIP and FIP... (to the rhythm of 'There was a fleet...')
I have always been a musical clown
I practise
And practice makes perfect

It's as simple as a musical phrase
Knowledge was a delight to my ear
My head was on the way
If I looked at myself
I saw myself twice
One that protected the other
And the other that gave the one
the feeling of rising
the feeling of pleasure
and the feeling of softly descending
enough for two
I glowed
I burned and burned
No bullshit could put it out
I turned blue
gave off light and shone
and left them in their delusions
After all, to them I was a lunatic
Sweet temptation
Sure babe, the moon was very large!
The Scheldt flooded
The rats were shocked
Anchors tore loose
Buoys floated away

It's not a game
It's neither losing or winning for myself
It's looking for the right colour
without denying who I am
I long for the right place
Where shall I carry my heart?
On my bottom?
Look, in one of the two right-hand chambers
there's a tissue nodule
that regularly ends in ignition
The nodule is the starter motor
This most tasty piece of flesh glows
and sees to it that the 2 left-hand chambers
and the 2 right-hand chambers contract
to pump the blood to the body and the lungs
The best quality...
It smells of children's shit
I'm a cannibal

I devour myself
And God saw that it was good (laughs)
And I practised
Practice makes perfect (laughs)

I'm glowing
as always
By concentration
By elimination
Yes, and by refusal too
My blood's gently boiling
My blood's flowing fast
I'm a volcano in a desert
In the desert of detachment
Isn't this a crafty creation?
Don't you write your own history?
Laughter
or a smile
Perhaps by me?
Perhaps for me?
I have an unceasing pain
between my shoulders
that I want?
I have a fever
that I want
37.4
It's a constant
When I was younger
I was already told, with a cautioning finger
I was told every day
"You live on the edge
You are a candle
burning at both ends
Calmness can save you"
I don't want to be calm
I'm burning
I'm a torch
in search of its eternal flight
I want to play with the law of gravity
I'll burn, go out and ignite
in the air
Even if there's no oxygen
So what?
I'm still burning
Even if I apparently do nothing
I burn more violently
than allowed and foreseen
I'm burning and not only for myself

but also to give others
light and fire
In the same way
I've received
light and fire from others
I have the fever
I'm a living torch
throughout my life
Through the hasty tempo of my singing
Sometimes a young crooner
Sometimes an old thief

(sings)
And now
The end is near
And so I face
The final curtain
My friend
I'll say it clear
I'll state my case
Of which I'm certain
I've lived
A life that's full
I've travelled each
And every highway
And more
Much more than this
I did it
My way (11)
...

The headache is on the way
back from being away
The fever has stayed, as always
Perhaps the fever of the pain
between my shoulders?
Or perhaps it's the fever of poor
authenticity? *(laughs)*
You can't buy it
It's there or it's not
And it has nothing
to do with that feverish banality
that remains from 2 clowns from another era
JEDER MANN IST EIN KUNSTLER (12)
EVERYBODY WILL BE FAMOUS FOR 10 MINUTES (13)
It's a banal reality
in your 24 hours of high-speed sleep
It's not a dream

You aren't dreaming
You don't have a fever
Appearances deceive themselves
Lies are told
temporarily reliably and quickly
You know what they
say nowadays
"Just act normally
then you'll be crazy enough"
It's a time
of schol proost and down the hatch
Because what people yesterday
with a lot of fuss
and bravos
and encores
and publicity
sold to the buyer
today turns out to be obsolete
and tomorrow past its time
It goes faster
than fast
Nowadays eternity lasts a second
For me the second will be an eternity
The second of the birth
an always, without pain
Perhaps my eternity lies
in my activity?
The search for permanence
Is permanence only possible
on the other side of the grave
Is that why I cut
my heart out of my body
and ate half of it?
I'll carry my heart between my legs
I'll feel it
It will happen
I sense that the feelings from both sides
will meet each other
It seems as if something between my shoulders
wants to greet you and me
Like an act of the
weightless body
or of a feather-light animal
That's why I practise
And practise makes perfect
Where is that ant?
It's here
What a bad joke

There's no refusal
Only acceptance
Broken mirrors celebrate triumphs
Through the bankruptcy of so-called culture
it rains new manifestos
From left to right
and right becomes left
Crushed philosophies
dangerous theories
fatal strategies (14)
And all those gamblers, in their striving
not to seem like each other
look exactly like each other
The opportunist drowns in the unique
Today's theory kills
Because our time is so much imprisoned
under the spell of mortality
that we have become desperate
and try to dope ourselves
We mix and adulterate everything with
the poison from several rats
so as not to notice that everything is perishing
Lancelot is here
disguised as an ant
I'm the knight of despair
When all the rivers flood
I'm the drunkard and I drown
When all the anchors break
I'm the smith and I burn
When all the buoys drift away
I'm the rescuer and I lose my way
When all the mirrors lose their reflection
I'm the leader and I'm not myself
Don't I have a heart?
Or is it as light as a feather?
Perhaps I'm a naughty child with faults?
Can I be anything else?
Yes, I can be an all-embracing catastrophe
I want to undergo the change
Otherwise there'll be a lack of disasters
due to an excess of goodness
Yesterday's theory is complaining
And perhaps becomes tomorrow's theory?
If the living know no refusal
the dead still refuse
Invisible but effective
in this damned circus
I practise in this tent

where everything has to succeed
and nothing may fail
Watch out! I'm practising!
Practice makes perfect

As you see
I don't have much skill
I don't have much wisdom
But my inner strength
if I may put it like this
is groping in the dark
Because everything I know
and I don't know much
I have discovered or experienced myself
From simple little failures
that you acquire yourself, you grow nicer
sadder and you become funnier
than from something huge you've only heard about

I don't want to be sad
I just want to be happy
Perhaps I want to be the audience?
Who am I now?
Who am I who so impudently
and mercilessly judges others
–who are perhaps my audience–
and asks them clumsy questions?
I'm still nothing
Where is that ant?
Gone
Lost its way
No, it's here
It doesn't bother me
that I spend my performances
in misery and have to wait
till I dream the unsolvable dream
The hereafter will ease it
That's the least I can
expect from that dream
My waiting, that restriction
will later become someone else's
moment of openness
and thereby despise and contest
the pettiness of accepting everything
Even if there's no laughter this evening
the laugh I wish to leave behind will still
spread out through time and space
be audible

to those who need it
My life should approach the perfection
of the unstoppable laugh
I may have what it takes
I possess the angelic rage
I possess the butterfly-like aggression
childish anarchy
and yearn for the glory and the colours
of powerlessness
There was a fleet that sailed to Spain
When it returned it came again
There was a crow sat on a stone
he flew away and there was none
I can dream the unsolvable dream
Surmise the supreme pleasure
Feel the sublime pleasure
Know the ultimate pleasure
Because I feel something changing inside
Will I feel the pleasure of the other
for whom I long?
Do I belong among those people who
in their attitudes,
belong together?
Perhaps in an institution?
There's lucidity
There's a lightness
Do I possess the weight of my heart?
It seems as if something
is beginning to push, to wrench, between my shoulders
That something is breaking out of my body
to speak
Is this the moment at which my dream
and my body touch each other
Would it work after all?
I know the extra value of waiting
but also the loss of the night
If I carried my heart on my back
would it work?
Perhaps it will never work
Aren't I the emperor of loss?
Is the ant still here?
Yes, here
Yes, it's still here
Or is it a caterpillar?
Have a look
I'm practising
And practice makes perfect

Didn't it work well?
Wasn't it pleasant?
No?
I, the clown of the evening
and of the night
that'll be coming soon
You may find it comical
But I want to move you
the audience
and carry you away
to another side of time
I want to make you
the audience
laugh and cry
on the other side of your being
But I see there's a problem
I don't understand any of it
Of the magician I used to be
Is there between us
more than only strangeness?
Is the aloofness disdain?
I don't know
Perhaps I've lost touch with you
the audience
or you, the audience
have lost touch with me
That happens quite often
It's all in the game
It can happen
Can it change?
Because without an audience
the clown dies
That's why I'm here
without refusal
I sensed it
I feel it
It's going to happen
In your eyes I'll be an idiot
You don't believe it
I feel it
It's going to happen
I'll accept that
without any form of refusal
What I suspected is happening
I no longer need to dream
my unsolvable dream
You don't have to laugh anymore
I feel it

I'm beginning again
Yes, I want to begin again
I feel it growing
In your eyes I'll be an actor
I'll know the secret
of every pleasure individually
Yes, I can still feel it growing
Everyone enjoys themselves separately?
I don't anymore
I' ll enjoy
for both
and for everybody
The supreme pleasure has begun
The sublime pleasure is on the way
The ultimate pleasure is here
The pleasure of the metamorphosis
The metamorphosis...
I'm beginning again
and shall see, hear and feel
new things
always and anew
I let someone else begin
In your eyes I really will be a clown now
But I don't care
Because I suspect
that wings
are growing between my shoulders
Now I'm sure of it
Wings are growing between my shoulders
I'll know the laugh of both sexes
I don't need mirrors any more!
I'm there!
I'm complete
I exist
Just look
(*turns round and walks away*)

I'll just go back to the beginning
Seek out the future
Life, the moon...
Fly around a bit, angrily, in the night...
(of that timeless engine room with pipes,
valves, stopcocks, pressures, speeds
Everything under intense pressure working with faultless
perfection and endless repetition)

◆

THE KING OF PLAGIARISM

Jan Fabre, 1998 - 2005

English translation by Gregory Ball

For my father,
the day he died
Langkawi, Malaysia, 15 January 2005

Sources / notes

Inspired by the work of the scientists John Brockman and Edward O. Wilson.
With thanks to HUMO for the title The King of Plagiarism and to the
Hersenstichting Nederland.

[1]   Devil in Disguise, Elvis Presley, written by Giant, Baum & Kaye
[2]   Albert Einstein
[3]   Charles-Maurice de Talleyrand-Périgord
[4]   Strawberry Fields Forever, The Beatles, written by Lennon & McCartney
[5]   William Shakespeare
[6]   William Shakespeare, The Tempest, Act IV, scene I
[7]   William Shakespeare, Macbeth, Act V, scene V
[8]   Leszek Kolakowski
[9]   William Shakespeare
[10] William Shakespeare, King Richard II, Act III, scene II
[11] After Jean-Luc Hennig in Apologie du plagiat
[12] Bloody Rotten Audience, Tony Miles
[13] Philippe Quinault
[14] Herman Teirlinck

MONOLOGUE FOR A MAN

(backstage)
It's so typical of chattering apes
to arrange a meeting in a theatre
Great
It's the house
where chattering apes
celebrate their apishness
And here, where drama feels at home
I have to prove
that I'm ready for the stage
Not easy
I've practised a lot
I've rehearsed a lot
And here where comedy belongs
I have to justify myself
Which brain shall I use to do that?
I don't have a brain
And here, where tragedy is life
I have to defend myself
Because I want to fill my emptiness
and want to give up my immortality
If the solution isn't simple
God won't provide the answer

Ah, a mechanical eye
Are the chattering apes watching me?
Could they be studying me?
Yes, I think so
Do you think they can hear me?
Perhaps I'm just a simple soul...
who feels good in a small group?
I would like
to thank you
the chairman and the members of the board
and the friends of the chairman
and the friends of the board
and the friends of the members of the board
and the friends of the friends of the members of the board
in advance
for letting me come here
to be heard
The red light isn't flickering anymore
Do you think they've stopped
observing me
filming me?
Perhaps I'm already famous?
Am I ubiquitous but elusive?
Do I seek the lights

only to hide in them?
Or am I anonymous
and already forgotten?
It's possible
Because for chattering apes
the time for coming and going
dashes at great speed
Because their time is limited
but very enjoyable
Maybe it's typical
of the time they live in?
What time is it?
Sssssshhhh
It's time
to try to pretend
Concentrate!
Go on and appear
but make sure you don't disappear.

(comes on and sings softly)

I look like an angel
I walk like an angel
I talk like an angel
But I got wise
I'm a devil in disguise
Oh yes, I am
A devil in disguise [1]

I realise...
The more sins I commit
the more chance
I can become a saint
A saint of the theatre
A saint who believes
in fabrications
and in pretending
A saint who can give himself
to the audience
Who can sacrifice himself
to the audience
To you

(he sings)
I look like an angel
I walk like an angel
I talk like an angel
But I got wise

... and I have a problem
I can't create anything
Because I know nothing of evolution
I'm...
I'm the subservient and the sterile self
that shuts itself up in its own originality
Am I alright here?
I can't do anything about it
I'm perfect
I'm unique
I'm rational
I'm wise
Or should I stand here?
I'm forward-looking
I'm long-suffering
I'm magnanimous
Can you hear me alright?
I'm unselfish
I'm honest
I'm sexless
and innocent
I'm a little nervous
Am I articulating well enough?
The Divine Engineer chose
to design me in his image
Odd, isn't it?
And if the solution isn't simple
God won't give any answer
You can be sure of that

I have a problem
And I'm fed up with it
As fed up as with playing the lyre in heaven
I don't want to be sterile
I don't want to be original
I don't want to be perfect
I want the loose ends of failure
Of wanting something
but not being able
but still keeping on trying
and not giving up
Is the colour of my skin alright?
I don't want to be unique
I don't want to be rational
I don't want to be wise
I don't want to be forward-looking
I don't want to be long-suffering
I don't want to be magnanimous

There in the back row, can you hear me alright?
I don't want to be unselfish
I don't want to be honest
I don't want to be sexless
And I want to be guilty of...
Of what?
Of what?
Of everything!
I have the feeling I'm standing in semi-darkness
Am I standing in the light?
Can you see my eyes properly?
Because I want to prove
justify
defend
my right to stand here
I think I have the strength
to change
I want the supreme feeling
And I want to have at my disposal
the blessing of fillability
How shall I achieve that?
It's something...
that has to grow organically
I'll study it here
with you
Yes, I have my doubts
But if we knew what we were doing
we wouldn't call it a study, or would we? [2]
(he examines)

That's what
has to happen here
That's what I want to achieve here
Living communication
that frees spiritual energy

I want to become an animal
A worm, no, not a worm!
I want to be an animal
that's put itself together
–just like the rest of this earthly life–
A chattering ape
An inspired genius
with animal cunning and emotion
Am I expressive enough?
I want to be one of you!
I want to be a man
who is fascinated

–like everyone–
by life
and even more so by death
And who is blessed
with boundless imagination
I want to be one of you
I want to be a human
and occasionally stupid
I want to be a human
who sometimes can't see
any further than the end of their nose
I want to be a human
who occasionally shits themselves
and is a coward
I want to be one of you
Why?
Because you are unpredictable
That's why people are better
than angels
And I ought to know
because I'm an angel
But not much longer
because I'm going to change
Do you want to know what time it is?
(he looks at one of his watches)
It's exactly 11:59 and 59 seconds
An original Dior
Perfectly imitated

Do I too have the talent
to be funny?
People are better than angels
because they have earned
the goodness they possess
with that complex but fragile organ
between their ears
on a long and hard journey
Your brain is the fruit
of millions and millions of years
of trial and error
Of wanting to
but not being able
but keeping on trying anyway
and not giving up
Your brain is a world
in itself
I want a brain like that too
And that's why I have brought the 'Steine' with me

Yes, I have brought some stones
I chose the best ones
At least, I think I have
You can never be 100% certain
But...
If we knew what we were doing
we wouldn't call it an inquiry, or would we?
(*he examines*)

Am I articulating well enough?
Don't forget: project!
Can you see and hear me well enough?
I still have a little stage fright, you see.
That will soon go!
But what do you expect?
Normally no one
sees or hears us
If thirty angels have an argument
or a party up on a roof
they make so little noise
that even an experienced observer passing the house
will not hear them and will miss them completely
whereas chattering apes communicate
ceaselessly with lots of noise
It's much easier to get them talking
than to keep them quiet
Maybe I'm just a naïve fool.
I don't know anymore
Or am I really so simple-minded?
A tongue isn't worth much without a brain
That's why I want the supreme feeling
and I want to adapt to
the blessing of fillability
I'm open to everything
Maybe that way I can belong somewhere?
I'd really like to have friends
So we can always tell each other the same things
I'd really like to have true friendship
The gateway to betrayal
So we can accuse each other
of your story being mine
and my story being his
Can I be friends with you?
Do you want to know what time it is?
(he looks at one of his watches)
Time is like a whore
She sleeps with everyone
It's 3 hours and 8 minutes and 30 seconds

As good as a real Cartier

I'm certain
that my wings are disappearing
I'm starting to feel the effect of gravity
I just can't keep quiet
You can hear it
I could be a chattering ape
I want to be one of you
I want to be a human
who believes in the lie
of man
I've practised
or rather I've rehearsed
communicating like you
I'm not good enough yet
Give me time
I want to be a human
I want to be the human
that you need
For anyone who wants to laugh
I'll be a comedy
For those who want to cry
I'll be a tragedy
For those who...
I still haven't found a sentence structure
for the word 'drama'
one that rolls off the tongue
Let me keep on looking
I've rehearsed that
sort of text a lot
In German theatres rehearsing is called
'proben'
Nice word, isn't it?
No, don't get me wrong
I don't want to be a German
But I think it's nice
Rehearse, 'proben', probe
When I probe, I'm rehearsing too
and then I also examine
how I can do something best
or how I can discover something
I didn't know before
Sometimes I don't know either...
You understand what I'm saying, don't you?
You know more about it than I do, don't you?
But...
If we knew what we were doing

we wouldn't call it study, or would we?
(he examines)

Your language is marvellous
You've invented a language
so you can hide your thoughts
from each other better [3]
Wonderful!
Man shows his true creativity
when trying to hide
his sources
In which he never succeeds
And in the attempt discovers
his deepest desire
Which he never succeeds in either
because he dies too soon
and likes eating strawberries far too much

(he sings)
Let me take you down, 'cause I'm going to Strawberry Fields
Nothing is real and nothing to get hung about
Strawberry Fields forever. [4]

I want mortality!
But I'm not a human yet
nor am I an angel anymore
So what quasi divine animal am I?
No, not a worm!
Maybe I'm just a simple fool?
That's why I've already been observing you
for millions and millions of years
I admire your existence
And I'm just a little jealous of your species
You see, all new feelings
I never had as an angel
I saw
and I still see
how you imitate one another
Penetration after penetration
Generation after generation
How miraculous it is...
that after their birth babies laugh and cry
And from the moment they can see
they start to imitate
adults' complex facial expressions and hand movements
Apes ape apes
I was there and I missed it
Or did I watch it?

Oh, the memory, the guardian of the brain [5]
That wasn't mine either
I'm doing well
I'm starting to talk more
using other people's words
Yours
Apes ape apes
I was there and I just watched it!
That quality is the germ
of all your education
and strategy
From cradle to grave
you learn to do
what you see others do

Our revels now are ended. These our actors,
As I foretold you, were all spirits, and
Are melted into air, into thin air
And, like the baseless fabric of this vision
The cloud-capp'd towers, the gorgeous palaces,
The solemn temples, the great globe itself,
Yea, all which it inherit, shall dissolve,
And, like this insubstantial pageant faded,
Leave not a rack behind. We are such stuff
As dreams are made on; and our little life
Is rounded with sleep. [6]

What did you think of it?
I brought a lot of stones with me
I'll hand some of them out
If I haven't been good enough
you can stone me
But wait a moment
Give me another chance
It may go better after a couple of rehearsals
In the German theatre rehearsing is called
'proben'
Don't get me wrong
I don't want to be a German
Let me rehearse
Let me figure it out
I know, I'm still hesitating a bit
Hesitation is in the nature of the beast
No, I'm not a worm
I'm a chattering ape
who's trying and seeking
What's the problem?
Aren't I allowed to seek it out?

I've been observing you
for millions of millions of years
I admire your species
And I'm a little jealous of your species
I want to know
the dangerous nuances of art
I saw
and I still see
how, at intervals of centuries
with a jubilant and fearful
but valiant heart,
the first chattering apes
draw over the same drawings
on the same rock faces
How, at intervals of several years
with a jubilant and anxious
but imaginative heart,
contemporary art apes
paint over the same paintings
on the same canvases
And whenever these pictures
are drawn over, painted over or copied
with a difference of a few centimetres
these chattering apes
are born over and over again
so as to function in new rituals
in which they celebrate the beauty of their mortality

And all our yesterdays have lighted fools
The way to dusty death. Out, out, brief candle!
Life's but a walking shadow, a poor player
That struts and frets his hour upon the stage,
And then is heard no more; it is a tale
Told by an idiot, full of sound and fury,
Signifying nothing. (7)

I thought it wasn't bad
You don't have to applaud
Only when it's very good
I'll hand out a few more stones
Large and small
You don't have to be shy
If you think I'm no good,
just stone me!
I've brought 4 special stones too
The first stone
The second stone
The third stone

And the fourth stone
Splendid fossils with billions of nerve cells
Billions of butterflies of the soul

Should I run through the text again?
Let me try again
It makes me very vulnerable, but that's really quite
interesting!
That's what it's like being a saint of the theatre
A rehearsal that the audience witnesses
In German theatres rehearsals are called
'Probe'
Don't get me wrong
I don't want to be a German
Let me seek it out
If we knew what we were doing
we wouldn't call it study, or would we?
(he examines)

It's a tale
Told by an idiot, full of sound and fury,
Signifying nothing.

Any contemporary philosopher
or scientist
or writer
who has never had the feeling
that he is a charlatan
must be a superficial soul
whose work is probably
not worth reading (8)
That's not mine either
It's going well
I'm increasingly starting to speak
in someone else's words
Because I want to be a charlatan
A sort of Columbus
More courage than knowledge
Balls, no, I haven't got any yet
That'll turn out alright
You'll see it will
I want the supreme feeling
The supreme feeling is believing
I want to have the blessing
of fillability at my disposal
I want to be human
But one who pretends
and thereby lives more intensely

The sharpening of my
physical reflexes is necessary in order
to be violent and expressive here
That's why I've been observing you
for millions of millions of years
I admire your species
And I'm a bit extremely jealous of your species
I saw
and I still see
how your loves and wars
begin and end with words
How you analyse and explain
nature and theory in figures
How you plagiarise each other's
words and figures
as much as you like
to improve
and to test each other
And the funniest thing is...
that you're not the only intelligent species on earth
But you are the only one that's so stupid
as to test and measure each other's intelligence
in words and figures
Nice people
People close to my heart
Am I a simple soul?
Because my brain doesn't feel it yet
although my heart can think it.
What do I have to do?
Carry on
Don't give up
Keep on trying, keep on looking
It's a good sign
I'm losing my lightness
I'm on the way from angel
to scamp
Do you want to know what the time is?
(he looks at one of his watches)
It's time to become human
and to realise that we're monsters
It's 16 hours and 22 minutes and 6 seconds
An original imitation, a Dior
Has anyone ever seen a real Dior?
Do they actually exist?
And if they existed
Who would wear such a thing?
Worms?
I saw

and I still see
how philosophers, scientists and writers
justify their plagiarism
and rightly so
They use writings they take like little children
from a bad environment
to introduce them into another, better environment (9)
They use mathematical theorems which they hide
like small birds in eagles' armpits
so they can reach the heights
they never could under their own power
By plagiarism you endorse each other's existence
or try to erase each other
Through plagiarism words and figures
are reborn again and again
to survive as a different value
in new performances
in which you crown the splendour
of your mortality
I want to be that other value
I want that crown
If I become
who I want to become
I can be anyone
A scientist, a philosopher, a writer
A doctor, a monster, a worm
A chattering ape, a human
An emperor of loss
A servant of beauty
A king of plagiarism

And nothing can we call our own but death
And that small model of the barren earth
Which serves as paste and cover to our bones.
For God's sake, let us sit upon the ground
And tell sad stories of the death of kings;
How some have been deposed; some slain in war,
Some poison'd by their wives: some sleeping kill'd;
All murder'd: for a hollow crown. (10)

You may clap your hands
It's an old tradition, after all
Show some sort of respect
A gesture of thanks
You may do anything, but you don't have to
Have you got enough stones?
I don't deserve any better if I'm no good
Start throwing!

Shall I give you some more stones?
What do you want; big ones or some pebbles?
I do want to keep on trying
and not give up
Like you
We angels always have to be sterile, original, perfect,
unique, rational, wise,
forward-looking, long-suffering,
magnanimous, unselfish, honest,
sexless and innocent
in everything we do
And you can see where that leads
Here I stand
I'll prove, justify and defend
the fact that I too can
ape
plagiarise
copy
imitate
It doesn't matter
what you call it
It is something natural
You use it to live
to correct
to expand
or to improve life
I hope I can be as good as you
I hope I can be human
I'll die
as a human
What a wonderful existence

As I said before
I've brought some special stones with me
Four brilliant caverns of the human mind
The first stone is that of a scientist
The second stone is from a writer
The third stone is from a philosopher
And the fourth stone is from a doctor
These brains are gigantic puzzles
But puzzles are there to be solved
by a future brain
By me!
I see some of you are looking astonished
What did you say? Impossible?
Impossible?
Impossible?
Impossible only means

that you haven't found the solution yet
If we knew what we were doing
we wouldn't call it study, or would we?
(he examines)

Just let me do it
I'll prove
that I can be one of you
But without common sense
Because common sense is no more than
a collection of prejudices
And that's not the sort of brain I want
Boss in my own brain
Boss in my own brain
(he repeats this until he wilfully makes a mistake)
Boss in my own belly
You see, I also have the talent
to be someone
of the other sex
I devoted some 'Probe' to it
I see some of you looking oddly
when I use that word
'Probe'
You see
Don't get me wrong
I don't want to be a German

I've brought with me the four most marvellous brains
The four ultimate temples
Together, these four stones
are your consciousness
The consciousness of modern man
Let me introduce you
These are the four 'Steine'
Einstein
Gertrude Stein
Wittgenstein
and Frankenstein

The supreme feeling is believing
And I'll have
the blessing of interpretability
And I'll conform to
the blessing of interpretability
I want to be a human
And as you can see
I have built the structure of my temple
I have made the upper part

out of eight different bones that will protect my temple
against the worst shocks and blows
Inside I have installed three membranes
and added fluid
so that my temple can float in the skull *(taps his head)*
gently and agreeably
A cork soul
and you float to the surface
If we knew what we were doing
we wouldn't call it an examination, or would we?
(he examines)

This is the brain of the physicist
Albert Einstein
I'm going to use several parts of his temple
to lay the foundations of my own
Pieces of his outer folds and cerebral cortex
from both his left and his right halves
Here lies the intellect
I'll be able to ape as well as anyone
with an understanding of things
and with endless curiosity
Einstein made us see
– I may, er, say 'us'
as that makes it easier to empathise –
He made us see
that reality is a theory
Invented, in other words
And that every view of nature
is a mathematical one
And that we cannot experience space with our senses
but only by carrying out a mental action
So the universe does not exist
It just is
It is just an invention

I'll be more of a human than the scientist
whom I ape
Because I have mastered 'aping' better
than the person I ape

And again and again
second by second
something changes in our minds
And after death we live on borrowed time
My skull is ready to contain about 1.5 litres
Yes, yes, you heard right
There is still room

Lots of room
I admit
I've already handled them
Two of the four 'stones' I brought with me
I couldn't keep my hands off them
I have to watch out
I could get addicted to them
Of course
I have already touched them
before I arrived at the theatre
Otherwise I couldn't be here
and move and speak like you
Because an angel has no brains
I have already told you
but you didn't believe it
because you like eating strawberries too much

(he sings)
Living is easy with eyes closed, misunderstanding all you see
It's getting hard to be someone but it all works out,
it doesn't matter much to me
Let me take you down, 'cause I'm going to Strawberry Fields
Nothing is real and nothing to get hungabout
Strawberry Fields forever. (4)

You listened properly, didn't you?
Please keep up your attention
My existence here is by your grace alone
If you –my audience– don't watch or listen
I'll never be able to become what I want
And what I want to become isn't only a vital choice
but a political one too
Because I want to defend the beauty
and the vulnerability of man
Standing here has consequences to
I suppose I sound like an old fool
from a different era, don't I?
Perhaps I really am an idiot
The capacity of my skull is a little larger
Normally
As you know
the normal capacity of the skull is 1.3 litres
In my case it's 1.5 litres.
I have 20 centilitres more space in my skull
Pure chance
A construction error
I think I used two bones too many
to make my skull

What do you think?
That I've got water on the brain?
But you know that the best inventions
occur by accident

Do you want to know what time it is?
(he looks at one of his watches)
It's time to plant
It's time to pick what you have planted
It's 3 hours and 38 minutes and 14 seconds
An original duplicate, a real Labrador
I thought a Labrador was a dog
A watchmaker's dog
If we knew what we were doing
we wouldn't call it study, or would we?
(he studies)

The second 'Stein' is a real 'Stein'
It is a female stone
Because without particles from a female brain
there can't be a proper marriage of reason and intuition
That explains the brain of the writer
Gertrude Stein
From her temple
I'll borrow the highly hormonal and linguistic elements
to elegantly decorate my temple
With a tuft of female flair
and with extreme refinement I'll be able
to plagiarise everything I need
Stein made us see
– I can say 'us'
as it makes the empathy more credible –
She made us see
that language is a re-creation
An intellectual re-creation
– an invention, therefore –
by means of the principle of repetition
By repeating words and phrases
she negated and denied
the meaning and the visualisation of meaning
Language is a universe
that refers only to its own inventions
A worm is a worm is a worm

I definitely want to possess her brainstem
She will make me a man
Motives and pleasurable feelings are produced
in the brainstem

And as you surely know
the brainstem is shaped like a penis with balls
I'll not give her brainstem to my temple
but carry it in the right place
I want to be a human
with the genitals of a genius
It will certainly boost my sex-appeal
And that's a welcome bonus
If I want to speak with my body more
I have to be able to seduce a little, don't I?
Can I try it out on you?
A rehearsal
In German theatres that's called 'Probe'
I think it's a nice word
Don't get annoyed
Don't get me wrong
I don't want to be a German

I'll be more of a human than the writer
who is plagiarised by me
Because I have a better command of plagiarism
than the person I'm plagiarising

And the person from whom I've borrowed
will be very grateful to me
Because the plagiarised author will flare up with rage
and will use the best of himself
to publicise his outrage
and let hypocrisy triumph
Do you hear that command of the language?
Thanks Gertrude!
His bitterly maligned honour
The exploitation of his authenticity
An attack on his original personality
And what else can he or she think up
In all that screaming and that fuss
just one thing is clear
The pure desire for recognition
of the plagiarised writer (11)
of the plagued writer
He or she simply wants to say
'I exist
I'm more of a writer
than the writer who plagiarises me
Because I have a better command of plagiarism
than the person who stole from me
I'm the king of plagiarism!'
Marvellous, isn't it?

Just as people help each other on
Praise each other to the heavens
Only people can do that
People remain in movement
Angels always hover in the same place
They're static
Dull, I can tell you all about it
That's why I want to be a human
and be able to die
Dying is part of movement
It's not standing still
I want to be a human
because dying is the nicest thing
that can ever happen to me
Because then your friends
or perhaps even you
have to arrange everything for me
Suppose I die
You have to take care of my body
The theatre of death commences
The coffin is chosen
and the cemetery arranged
The suit I have to wear is tailored
and I'm made-up
so I make a splendid appearance
You, my friends, say a lot
of positive things about me
It is a great and overwhelming success
And touchingly sentimental
because everyone cries for me
I'd like to help
but I can't
because I'm dead
(he smiles)
I'd like to know
all the things I'll do as a human
What parts I'll play
and how I'll die onstage
That's if I get out of here alive, at least
and am not battered by stones
But there we are...
If we knew what we were doing
We wouldn't call it study, or would we?
(he studies)

The third stone, er... 'Stein', er... stone
is the brain of the philosopher
Ludwig Wittgenstein

I'm going to plunder his temple too
to create my temple
That's the good thing about a human
You die
And one's man's death is another man's breath
I'll use his Corpus Callosum
the main connection between the two hemispheres
so that my intelligence spreads
quickly and easily
from the left half of my brain to the right half
and from the right half of my brain to the left half
And back, of course
And back, of course
And back, of course
And back, of course
And back, of course
I'll be able to copy anything I choose
at neuronal speed and with cunning agility
–because philosophers are cunning–
Wittgenstein made us see
–I can say 'us'
as it makes the empathy more genuine –
He made us see
that what we cannot speak about,
which we cannot therefore invent
must be communicated in silence
But that's what's so good about us
We can't be silent
We are chattering apes, aren't we? *(laughs)*
The boundaries of our language
are also the boundaries of our world
of our universe

I'll be more human than the philosopher
who is copied by me
Because I have a better command of copying
than the person I copy

And again and again
from second to second
something changes in our minds
And we live after death on borrowed time

Do you want to know what time it is?
(he looks at one of his watches)
You've lost time
somewhere between sunrise and sunset
A golden minute

inlaid with 60 diamond seconds
And they have vanished forever
It's 18 hours and 17 minutes and 59 seconds
It's high quality, Japanese imitation, a Seiko

(the angel looks at its body)
My body's becoming more and more physical
I'm doing well
It's typical
if you're doing well
God's on your side

If I'm fully accepted by you
And if I'm pleased with the qualities of my appearance
I'll rehearse even more in the future
'Probe' even more
Don't get me wrong *(irritated)*
I don't want to be a German
Why don't I want to be a German? *(angry)*
There is that great German soul
Johann Wolfgang Von Goethe
who always says
'Everything intelligent has already been thought of
One must only try
to think of it again oneself'
Why should I bloody well try to be original?
Why aren't I bloody well allowed to use anything?
And waste time and energy thinking up
what has already been thought up
In my temple I want to
study and fantasise about
why we think what we think
If we knew what we were doing
we wouldn't call it study, or would we?
(he examines)

The fourth 'Stein'
The most important of all stones
is the brain of Dr Victor Frankenstein
His brain, a superior artificial gift
of human ability
The artistic gift from the chattering apes
to themselves
Bravo, bravo, bravo! *(he applauds)*
I salute
this temple
with all due respect
I'll strip

this temple bare
I'll take everything from the first part of the brain
The complete R-complex of the left and right halves
the part with which we maintain life
and provide for one of the most elementary needs:
protection against friend and foe
Very important to me
because I'll arouse a lot of jealousy
with my temple
Make a lot of enemies
and lose a lot of friends
I'll be able to imitate everything
when and where I want
with boundless energy
but with precision too
Frankenstein has made us see
–Yes, I say 'us'–
that he is the inventor of artificial intelligence
Mankind formulates theories
and himself
according to his own image
So man devises inventions
and invents himself according to his own inventions
I'm a chattering ape
And we chattering apes
formulate theories based on
other theories
They are all inventions
that are speculative
and we therefore have no notion
of what we are creating
All theories,
all inventions, are Frankenstein monsters
I'm an invention
but I'm a fine playful monster
What naivety makes me believe
I'll be loved?
I have the blessing
of interpretability
I'm an invention
I'm an actor!
Because I believe
that the human form
is the supreme expression of the divine
And yet...
Odd?
And yet I'm starting to despise mankind
What naivety protects me

from the hostile outside world?

(he sings angrily)
Well, here's a song I've written specifically for you
Who sit in the audience and talk through all I do
I cannot understand it 'cause I'm pretty good, you see
So there must be something wrong with you
There's nothing wrong with me

You're a bloody rotten audience whilst I am very good
If brains were made of oak and ash
then you'd have balsa wood
I'm ethnic and authentic and I'm really full of class
While you're ignorant, you're cultureless,
you're philistines en masse. (12)

I have to watch out
It's not wise
to be wiser than necessary (13)
Did you hear that?
Did I think it up myself?
How humanly pretentious
In my temple
my body has to shine
and die endlessly in the lights
embrace death like a final friend
Just let me do it
I've rehearsed it a lot
In German theatres it's called 'Probe'
I find that the right word
'Probe' – probe
Don't get me wrong
I don't want to be a German
Don't be disappointed
I really don't want to be a German!
Because Germans are always sterile
Always original
Always perfect
Always unique
Always rational
Always wise
Always forward-looking
Long-suffering
Magnanimous
Unselfish
Honest
Sexless
and never guilty

Have you got enough stones
to stone me with?
I'd be proud
to be able to die here as an actor
What could be finer
than giving your last breath
to your audience
I'd accept it as a triumph
to be killed here
to be stoned here

I'd like to thank you
the chairman and the members of the board
and the friends of the chairman
and the friends of the board
and the friends of the members of the board
and the friends of the friends of the members of the board
I hope...
that I've defended myself well
that I've given sufficient evidence
that I've given a clear account
May I stay
and be one of your species?
May the worms eat me?
I see your eyes saying 'yes'
Oh, I'm happy
I'll be the finest meal for them
The time has come
I exist
I'm seen and heard
THIS WORLD IS MY STAGE
I made that up myself!
I'm an actor
Perhaps I'm a replacement for... God? (14)
The supreme fabrication is...
is believing in a fabrication
And the truth is...
knowing that it's a fabrication and believing in it
Do you want to know what the time is?
(he looks at one of his watches)
It's time to judge
whether your time deserves this actor
or this time can count itself lucky it has me
It's 0 hours and 0 minutes and 15 seconds
Here, as a chattering ape,
I can celebrate my being an ape
I've imitated an indescribable amount
used others' ideas

copied images
reworked words and sentences
so much that I believe they are my own
I've become
what I've copied
Yes, I'm an actor
who thinks up his own lines
I'm a sponge
that absorbs everything
I'm a biological machine
that colours everything
I'm a myth
where every Tom, Dick and Harry live
I'm the labyrinth
where someone always finds their way
I'm a human
with all the shortcomings, weaknesses
and diseases that exist
I don't have a single original idea
I have nothing of my own
And when I delve deeper into myself
and my feelings and thoughts
unravel
there turns out to be nothing
An uncompromising apotheosis
Only a void

And again and again
second after second
something changes in our minds
And we live after death on borrowed time

I see my stupid
and naïve face
I accept the bliss
I exist as a shell
Have I been destroyed by my own ambition?
Or am I glorious as a result of my own being?

I'm back
to the start
to the beginning
What strange God
protects me from mankind?
I'm back among my own kind
An angel
who's seen by no one
who's heard by no one

and who has no territory

(the angel panics and starts shouting and screaming
but no one hears him)
I'm not unique
I'm not an angel
I'm not unique
I'm not unique
Why am I unique?
Aren't I convincing enough?
Am I a worthless actor?
He who has no guilt
cast the first stone
Isn't that what I thought?
Damn and damn and damn and blast it
Why am I unique?
(first one stone falls, then a rain of stones falls from heaven)
Typical: when the solution is simple
that's when God gives an answer
What did you say?
Me, a saintly idiot?
Why?
I don't understand
Repeat it once again
You-are-unique
if-you-want-to-imitate-others
but-you-don't-succeed

◆

THE SERVANT OF BEAUTY

Jan Fabre, 2004-2009 (Antwerp, Vis and Gstaad)

English translation by Gregory Ball

Sources / notes

Madame est servie, Diane de Keyzer, Van Halewyck nv, 1995.

L'anus solaire, essay by Georges Bataille, Galerie Simon, Paris, 1931.

[1] The French word patron is used throughout the play and is equivalent to the English 'boss', but generally with the connotation of 'owner', taking it closer to 'proprietor'.

[2] Neil Armstrong, when he took the first step on the moon: 'It's one small step for a man, one giant leap for mankind.'

[3] André Breton, from Nadja, Gallimard, Paris, 1928.

MONOLOGUE FOR A MAN

Good evening, my dear audience
I'm happy
to see you
and my intuition tells me
that you are glad to see me too
I shall perform for you as if it were the first time
Or as if it were the last time in my life
You will judge me, of course
But my dearest wish is that my employer
is contented after the show
His opinion is crucial to me
My employer is of vital importance to me
but he's defenceless
That's why I have to look after him
Protect him
Yes, even defend him
Do I possess that fearless valour?
Oh, that sounds old-fashioned
(scratches himself)
I think you don't always realise it
But it is you that let my employer
appear and disappear
My employer tells me
And also deceives me about a lot
Is there a fear of disillusion?
No, only an appetite for illusion!
In that way he gives me
lots of joy and energy
And that's why I'm standing here!
This play is an ode to my employer.
And I'm standing here
to proclaim
my manifesto
loud and clear
and in all modesty
to put my manifesto
into practice
(scratches himself)
Because this play–
which I wrote myself
and which I have to perform myself,
because I don't have anyone else
and because the style and the content
are not of this age–
is a manifesto!
(scratches himself all over)
This evening, before your very eyes,
I shall reach a state in which you will not be able to see me

A gifted genius without talent
And clear eyes without a body
(scratches himself all over)
Another part of my programme for this evening
is that I shall play
my two favourite acts for you
'The tragicomic appearance and disappearance of beauty'
After all, don't forget!
My theatre is a parody
And everything one observes
in my theatre
is a parody of something else
The marionette, for example, is a parody of the actor
(scratches himself all over)
Bonsoir cher publique (Good evening dear audience)
My name is
John Soup
I was born in the last century
In Antwerp
Well, that's a long time ago
I'm living in the wrong age
My theatre puppets first appeared
in the Middle Ages, en France
That's why they're called marionettes-à-fil (puppets on a string)
See, they hang on wires
They're so elegant
They're beautifully embellished pieces of wood
My employer
taught me
what sensuality is and what is pleasing
to the eye
And you can see that erotic aspect, can't you?
I made my marionettes-à-fil (puppets on a string)
with my own hands
I'm proud of them
They have a character
and a will of their own
They are physically adjusted
Move stiffly, but with finesse
Have one single expression
And they remain silent
They don't complain
when heads roll
Even when at work they don't discuss
the 'psychologie du personnage' (psychology of the character)
nor the 'sémiologie du spectacle' (semiology of performance)
They don't have any idiotic conservative ideas
about le theatre

They don't want to glorify themselves
and perform on the Cour d'Honneur every year
or exhibit in the Louvre
They have no public life
In other words
they are nothing at all like French actors
They are what makes it all worthwhile
(scratches all over)
What's the matter with me?
Have I got trouble with my nerves?
Or did I eat something I shouldn't have before the show?
I've already been working
for the same employer for forty years
I'm not even considering retirement
I'll stay with the same employer
until I die
Does the young generation
still have that sense of honour?
Sometimes I feel I don't belong in this age
What did you say?
If a cat was a cow I could milk it
So, a cheerful chappy in the audience!
Yes, I know
There are hardly any cows left
When we see a cow
it's a purple creature that's trying to look like a cow
and produces milk chocolate
John Soup, you're making a fool of yourself
Excusez-moi
I shouldn't behave
as if I were one of my marionettes-à-fil (puppets on a string)
I absolutely mustn't be so pretentious!
Anyway, that sense of honour, in my opinion it really exists!
I work for a good boss
I'd like to call him 'patron' [1]
For the French it's a compliment
And in this case quite sincere
My 'patron'
lacks reason
never compromises
He doesn't think in terms of profit
And when he took me on
he never asked whether I was
'bien propre et honnête' (clean and honest)
He accepted me
as I was
A little wretch with an imagination that's out of control
who wanted to be a puppeteer

I whore and belch
But I'm loyal
to my 'patron'
For my 'patron'
I would get down on my knees
Always submissive with pleasure
Always subservient with respect
And always polite
Monsieur est servi? (Are you being served, sir?)
As you've probably heard
I speak a little French
Picked up en cours de route (along the road)
I had to
Because my 'patron' is everywhere
He is even there where they speak French
(scratches all over)
The more I scratch
The more it itches
It's annoying
I'll introduce and manipulate
my most important marionettes-à-fil (puppets on a string)
Here they are
The three main characters
Number three! This marionette-à-fil is Marion
The prostitute
Une comedienne classique française (a French classical actress)
Number two! This marionette-à-fil is Marie
The virgin
Un paradoxe français (a French paradox)
And number one! This marionette-à-fil is Jean Potage
The hero and the fool
Une star et artiste français (a French star and artiste)
The floor is dirty
All footprints
I had expressly asked the technicians
not to walk over the stage anymore
after the floor had been cleaned
Respect for the artist
is a thing of the past!
I'll do it myself
(cleans)
You can see I've done this a lot
That's how I started
I went into service young
Yes, you language purists, I know
I don't speak proper English
But I do speak perfect dialect
(scratches all over)

Anyway, everyone in Flanders
and especially the old guard
knows what I mean by that
'Go into service' is the most commonly used official name
for an unofficial existence
Life in the service of...
Beauty
My 'patron' is beauty!
And tonight, before your very eyes,
I shall take the ultimate step
'C'est un petit pas pour l'homme, mais un pas de géant pour
l'humanité' ('It's a small step for a man, one giant leap
for mankind') [2]
I want to be neither
heir nor imitator
In the name of romanticism
the true avant-garde
I want the vital intensity
of a unique act
The step from an unofficial
to an invisible existence!
I shall justify my life
in the service of beauty
Oooooow!
Did you see that?
Jean Potage kicked me up the bum
Yes, Jean, I know
I haven't forgotten them
Et Maintenant (sings Gilbert Bécaud)
I shall introduce
and manipulate
my two most important supporting parts
Number two! This marionette-à-fil is The Ape
Un stagiaire Français (a French apprentice)
Disguised as a French poodle
And numéro un! This marionette-à-fil is the Grim Reaper
Death
Un comédien français qui pense
qu'il est un révolutionnaire (a French actor who thinks
he's a revolutionary)
Are my shoes dirty?
I can see everywhere I've walked and stood!
Wait a minute
I'm going to clean off the soles of my shoes
And clean the floor again
I admit
I have an incredibly strong urge
to perform in public

But this evening I don't want to leave any footprints
I don't want anyone
to notice that I've been here.
As a servant of beauty you have to be self-effacing, don't you?
Carrying out my unique act
which will happen in a flash
will also show my defeat!
I may even cry.
But perhaps my tears will glitter
like a victory!
(scratches all over)
I'm the nervous type
You've probably already noticed that
It's widely said and known
that where it itches you have to scratch!
It wears me out so.
Life is a parody
and everybody knows
that there's always another interpretation lacking
Getting older, for example, is a parody of youthful
exuberance
I was ten when I chose, intuitively,
to enter into service
I've never regretted it
Non, rien de rien
Non, je ne regrette rien (sings Edith Piaf)
I presented myself
as a garcon à tout faire (Jack of all trades)
Even then of course one had to go to school
I saw several schools from very close up
But they didn't look back at me
From fifteen to twenty I learnt to stare
at the Académie des beaux arts d'Anvers (Antwerp Academy
of Fine Arts)
But they were my least interesting years
Now I'm standing here
rhyming in verse without lifting my arse (laughs)
Do you think I'm a farcical figure?
No! I'm not as good as my marionettes
That wasn't an easy time
Because there was too little of everything
in my home
I soon experienced
that poverty is a provocation
I fled
again and again
to my 'patron'
And yearned inquisitively

for his strength and intelligence
His powerlessness and anarchy
His stubbornness and tenderness
By I also discovered his strictness
A new master
means new rules
but in my case
it meant a lot more than that
Absolutely everything was new
A new world opened up
I had a world to gain
My option for the future
A passion for reality
translated into an artistic act
Monsieur est servi? (are you being served, sir?)
The servant of beauty
is here
So, for you, my audience
The first act

MARIE
D'yer wanna look after me kid?
'Cos I wanna show the world
Them lovely fings
What you make

JEAN
Yeah, why not
As a real knight of beauty
I'll make sure no one touches yer kid
And if anyone tries, 'cos you never know in Belgium
I'll cut him down
An' if you give us a smacker
It'll all be fine and dandy
Come 'ere, give us a kiss
'Cos you're lovely, lovelier than lovely

MARIE
Jus' one kiss then
Seulement un baiser hein mon bijou (just a kiss, my sweet)
Don't forget I'm a virgin
I'm a good girl, me

JEAN
I wanna suck your titties too
An' lick that little pussy of yours

MARIE
I ain't got no pussy
I've only got a doggie
A French poodle
Alright then, give me tits a suck

JEAN
Oh you 'ave got nice titties
Can I eat 'em all up?
I'm starvin' 'ungry
'Cos I'm only rich as hell
inside me 'ead.
With all them nice fings
What I fabre-cate

MARIE
You mad?
Mad genius
Je suis très catholique (I'm very Catholic)
I'm off
Make sure you look after me kid
Like a knight of beauty should
I'm gonna do a good deed
I'm gonna tell Tom, Dick and Harry
What luvverly fings you make
Votre oeuvre est très special (You're oeuvre is very special)

JEAN
I may be mad
But only for you, hot bitch
Watch art or I'll make your virginity
Into a lady's purse

MARIE
I'm off
I don' wanna hear yer
or see yer anymore

(The child is crying all the time)

JEAN
I'm fed up being a maid
I'm a knight of beauty
That kid cries too much
I'm gonna make that kid
a sculpture
A coupla planks
A few nails

In the kid's paws
And another nail in his footies
It's done!
Bah, it's no good, that sculpture
I'll make it disappear

*(Jean throws the child up in the air and it doesn't
come down again)*

That's right
Now it's up there
From now on Marie's a real
Hot bitch
'Cos I've never seen
A virgin wiv a child

MARIE
Where's me kid?
What'you done wiv it?
Where's me kid? (panic, big panic)

JEAN
Come here, girlie
I'll give you an 'and
You're much too lovely
To nag too much
I'll give you a good seeing to
In every hole in your body

MARIE
Mais je suis une vierge (Oh, but I'm a virgin)

JEAN
I couldn't care less
'bout all those symbols
Je t'adore, je t'adore (I adore you, I adore you)
It's party-time, girl
An' we're gonna celebrate
I'll make you some new kiddies
Wiv me wedding tackle
Oh you're so lovely
It sends me blind

MARIE
Je suis une vierge (I'm a virgin)
Je parle Français (I speak French)
Et j'adore la beauté (I adore beauty)
Non, non, arête! (No, no, Stop!)

JEAN
I'll teach you to gabble in French
Stuck-up cow
I'll put yer eyes out
An' take you in your eye-sockets
There, na you can get off too
I'm doing 'im up there a favour
An' there ain't nuffin' nicer 'n
Doin' someone a favour
(*Marie ascends and The Ape appears*)

Ah, my mate The Ape
Disguised as a French poodle
Un stagiaire Français (A French apprentice)
Tryin' te speak dialect
You can learn a lot from us, you can

THE APE
D'you fink it's so great, 'eaven?

JEAN
Did I say that?
D'you wanna disappear too?

THE APE
No, but doncha fancy goin' to 'eaven?
Singin' all day
For him with 'is grey beard?
Behavin' yerself and linin' up
Cleanin' all our lyres 'n turnin' 'em up
An' painting pictures all the time
Of foeze cherubs
Or d'you go to 'ell?
Where yer can fuck all day
An' do everyfink what's not allowed
An' 'fabre-cate' all sorts of fings that'll make
steam come out a their ears in 'eaven
That's nice too, ain't it?
C'est très bon aussi, hé? (That's very nice too, isn't it?)

JEAN
You're a real conjuror's ape, ain't yer?
My intuition tells me
You're a French catholic poodle
I ain't goin' nowhere
Can't yer see that
I'm stayin' 'ere
I don' believe

In all that claptrap
All I believe in's beauty
I'm a knight of beauty
'Cos tomorrer I'got to look after
Marie's kiddie again
The virgin
Un paradoxe français (A French paradox)
An' later on I've gotta play with that
Lovely dove
Marion, the tart
Une comedienne classique française (a French classical actress)
She can move all 'er lips
An' she can give a French kiss
Up top an' down below
I don't wanna miss that
I 'ave to fink of me international career, don' I?

THE APE
Where?
In Antwerp?

JEAN
Stupid marionette!
First time I saw yer
I fought you was an ape
But my intuition told me you was
Un stagiaire français (a French apprentice)
Disguised as a French poodle what's blind

THE APE
I ain't no ape
I'm an 'uman made by 'im up there
An' who can see perfectly well
That what you do is all well fabre-cated

JEAN
Alright, let's forget it
One day you'll make a good marionette-à-fil!
I believe that
Say that Jean Potage
Said so
I'll have a chat with 'im upstairs

(*Lights out*)

Did you watch and listen
to my marionettes?
Did they get all your attention?

Did they catch all the light?
Or wasn't I sufficiently in the darkness?
I want to be even more in the background!
I want only my marionettes-à-fil to be visible!
(scratches all over)
Did anyone here bring some lice in with them?
Madam, are you itchy too?
And you too?
I can see several people scratching
What's going on here?
I want my marionettes
to be even more credible and sincere in the second act
So I have to make sure
that my mastery is no longer visible
I shall be an invisible master
in manipulating my instruments
I want my beloved creatures
to create unreal dimensions
Dramatic effects and dreams
that cannot be achieved
with human actors in a theatre
The world is a parody
and everybody knows
that another interpretation is always lacking
The eye, for instance, is a parody of God
Why is that?
The floor's covered in my footprints
Is there so much dust here?
Or are my soles giving it off?
I'll take off my shoes
Yes, that's better
Move about quietly, carefully
Then you don't leave any traces
I always have too much energy
(scratches all over)
Are they bites?
Or is my imagination playing tricks on me?
I know
I'm the restless type
Sometimes nervous
verging on delusion
Daytime doesn't usually satisfy me
The night occasionally brings me help
I continue delving unceasingly into myself
for the formula
I need
to go from the power of my imagination
to the ultimate power of reality

What did you say?
That's right, my imagination is unstoppable
But you don't have any imagination
Are you a scientist?
There are lots of you
with imagination tonight, aren't there?
Who use their imagination
to build castles in the air
Anyone who does that is a fantast
I'm not a fantast
I have imagination
I'm standing here
To give shape to my imagination
in honour of my 'patron'
Perhaps I'm a marionette-à-fil
and I'm being manipulated
and move through beauty
(sings chanson 'Comme une marionette sur un fil')

I'm standing here
and will surrender my body
to remain present
as a pair of eyes
of eternal clarity
that seem to float in space
Every one of you
thinks that someone who is invisible
can nevertheless still see
But according to science
someone who is invisible
would be blind
because his eyes can't absorb any light
nor reflect light
But scientists are accountants
they have no imagination
So I thought up the following
Before I use the invisibility formula on myself
I'll simply stick my eyes shut with tape
and from the moment I become invisible
Completely transparent
I'll pull the tape off my eyes
and my eyes will be visible again
and I'll be able to see again
Do you know why I look up to my 'patron'?
I admire his quest
His leap into the unknown
His vulnerability and durability
His subtlety and uselessness

Do I venerate my 'patron'?
Do I encourage him?
Yes, with deafening modesty
Because he has abolished calendars
and always enfeebles the medicine called 'wisdom'
Because he is a monster
who makes slavish minds fearful
Because he reflects the colour of freedom!
And do you know what I want to reflect?
Air!
I want to be just air
with alert and twinkling eyes in it
Eternal in their brilliance
That move onward in nothingness
and which reflect beauty
(scratches all over)
I've got such an incredible itching
all over my body
According to me, I've got...
I don't dare say it.
Have you got the same trouble?
Yes, I can see several people scratching.
I've always had good relations
with my 'patron'
I've spoken to him regularly
And have observed him a lot
I've got the impression
that he conceals an infinite number of intentions
and allows an infinite number of interpretations
He is unfathomable
and very lonely
Sometimes he doesn't want to communicate with the outside
world
But when he goes out in public
his essence shows up well like a poetic shock
and he shows us his perpetuity
his transience
Damn it all, what's all that?
Have my socks become so dirty?
Even now I'm still making marks
I'll take off my socks
That's better
Yes, my feet are clean
They don't sweat
so they don't leave any prints
I love
my 'patron'
And love is a form of faith

This faith in my 'patron'
makes for a readiness
to invest a lot
in risk-taking
Because I have confidence in mon patron (my patron)
I dare to use that French military term
I'm avant-garde *(pronounced as in French)*
The vanguard
Because I long
to live in another age
to lead an invisible existence
and simply to cover up my eyes
But there we are, I know
that term is timeworn nowadays
Not done
Passé
Out of fashion
It doesn't matter
I've never been in fashion either
Le mot français 'avant-garde' (the French word avant-garde)
Nowadays it even sounds pejorative
Yes, that's right!
The French army would have gone straight to fight in Iraq
if they'd been able to find truffles there!
Remember what that American general said
'I'd rather have a German army against me
than a French army with me'
Am I a marionette-à-fil
that's scoffing at itself?
That's making fun of the solemnity
of the performance?
Or am I in a representation of the past?
The emperor of loss
The king of plagiarism
Or am I in a representation of the future?
The god of the middle class
Who possesses the spark
that's looking for a powder keg?
I am avant-garde
I'm a one-man group
with marionettes
highly active without being organised
not aggressive or provocative
I want to make my rebellion visible
firstly by applying the invisibility formula to myself
secondly by means of my simple idea of the tape
I shall be two twinkling objects
Eternal in their brilliance

In every object
120 million light-sensitive cells
Small, spherical glistening cameras
in the ether
so that only my marionettes are visible
La marionette-à-fil super au pouvoir! (the super powerfull
puppet on an string)
(scratches all over)
What sort of bites are they?
What sucking parasites
are living off my blood?
They're drinking your blood too
Because I can see more and more of you scratching!
What have we got now?
Jean Potage
is pulling his own wires
Did you see that?
Doesn't he agree with me?
With his manipulator?
Don't I manipulate you well
or are you rising up
against your maker?
Or are you trying to tell me
that a master is no better than his servant
Monsieur est servi? (are you being served, sir?)
The servant of beauty
So for you, my audience,
The second act

   JEAN
Hello Marion
Hello me little pleasure dove

   MARION
Jean Potage, 'ave yer bin fabre-cating'
some more of that junk
Then I can drop me knickers
Ter sell that rubbish
That's wot I like doin'
It's me callin'
   JEAN
I don't make no junk
It's all nice fings

   MARION
But I can't see nuffink
'n if there ain't nuffink te see
I can't flog it, can I

JEAN
It's all in me 'ead
'n I'm gonna do summink wiv me body
A beautiful deed

MARION
A beautiful deed, indeed
You'd better do a good deed
Fabre-cate a bit of rubbish
Then I can flog it

JEAN
Luvverly pleasure dove
How much does it cost?
To use yer?
I really fancy a bit
En doin' what you fancy
That's what it's all about, ain't it!

MARION
I'm too dear for you
You ain't got enough for so much luvverliness

JEAN
Ain't I good enough for yer?
I'm a knight of beauty, ain't I?
'n anyway, we all come from monkeys

MARION
Not me, mate, I'm from La douce France

JEAN
I'd fancy bein' an 'ore too
'n I wouldn't ask much

MARION
You're an 'ore anyway
Yer sell me yer pretty fings
what yer fabre-cate, don't yer?
'n I flog 'em at an 'andsome profit
Ha ha ha.....

JEAN
Na, that's not wot I mean
I'd like ter sell me body too
I'd offer it real cheap
Like the sales

MARION
Wot'd you ask then?

JEAN
A bit a love
Two tits 'n a fanny

MARION
Oh, so cheap
Yer can be my 'ore then

JEAN
I'm ready fer it
Me intuition was right
Me body knew it
How d'yer want ter use me?
'Cos a good service
Is never lost

MARION
Ah mon amour (oh, my love)
Vous êtes un animal (you are an animal)
Baise-moi (fuck me)
'n you've gotta be my man
'Cos you're so good inside

JEAN
You're pretty nice inside too
I can feel it
A fanny's as soft as velvet
Ha, ho, ha, it's so good
Fer you too?

MARION
Oui mon amour (oh, my love)
Ha, ho, ha, I'm gonna explode
Who am I?
Wot kin' a creature 'm I turnin' into?

JEAN
Une comedienne classique française? (a French classical actress)

MARION
Ha, ho, ha, ho ho, ha ha, non
Non!

JEAN
Wotcha mean, no?

Yer not that stagiaire française (that French apprentice)
Disguised as a French poodle, are yer?
Oh well, it's not so bad
I wanted to 'elp that girlie too
Yer don't look like an ape anyway
Or 'ave yer disguised yerself
As une comedienne classique française?

MARION
Who am I?
Ho, ha, ho, ha
I'm losin' meself
Where am I?
Ho, ha, ho ha...

(Marion ascends and disappears)

JEAN
Damn, where's she gone na?
She's gone
Well, that's the limit
The best things don't last long
'n I adn't even come yet
With all that discoverin'
Wiv wot kin' of creature she was

THE GRIM REAPER
Jean, Jean?
Don' worry, I'll marry yer
'n I'll be yours forever
Je parlerai aussi français to yer (I'll speak French to you too)

JEAN
'ave yer gone mad
Ter think I'd marry yer
'n spend the rest of me life
lookin' after 'n protectin' yer I s'pose?

THE GRIM REAPER
A beautiful death
Yer can't ignore that
'n I've 'ad a good look
I know wot I 'ave to do
I can be a sweet little pleasure dove too
After all, I sleep
With everyone too

JEAN
Yer just
Un comédien français qui pense
Qu'il est un révolutionnaire (a French actor
who thinks he's a revolutionary)
But who's just too stupid and clumsy
Ter play anyone lifelike

THE GRIM REAPER
If yer wiv me
Them nice fings wot you make
'll be worf much more

JEAN
I ain't gonna fabre-cate nuffink fer money
It's inside me 'ead
I'm gonna do somefink wiv me body
A beautiful deed
I wanna just vanish

THE GRIM REAPER
If yer marry me
No one'll be able to see yer no more
Only me
'Cos yer so lovely

JEAN
'ere, take that
I'll put yer eyes out
Then yer won't see me no more
There, take that
That's the end of yer
Dead as a doornail!

THE GRIM REAPER
Yeah, I know (sad)
Are you angry wiv me, Jean Potage?

JEAN
No, it's alright
Don' worry about it

THE GRIM REAPER
Well, you did act that well
I was really taken in
I was completely convinced
Vous êtes une vraie star et artiste français (You're a real French
star and artist)

JEAN
Yeah, yeah, I bet!
There's just one fing I 'ope
That Marion's there nex' time
'Cos she really seems to 'ave vanished

MARION
Mais non, je suis ici! (No, I'm not, I'm here)
I can sell meself well, eh, sweetie
C'est tout! (that's all!)
'n anyway, real beauty
Never fades
I'm always visible!

I sensed it
I'm convinced of it
You watched and listened
only to my marionettes
I've almost reached my goal
Of simply covering my eyes with tape
I'll accept the oddness
that excludes all intimacy
I'll become immaterial
Invisible
(sings 'La marionette')
The body is a parody
and everybody knows
that there's always still another interpretation lacking
Like that, the brain is a parody of a cauliflower
(sings 'La marionette')

Do my feet sweat after all?
Or is it just through the weight of my body
that I leave footprints?
I'm doing the best I can
to keep the floor clean
See, it makes me cry
Do I have to chop off my feet?
Look, now I'm wiping off my own tears!
What am I to do?
To start with I'll dry my feet
That may help a bit
(scratches all over)
According to me I've got fleas
You get that sometimes in these theatres
Especially in the ones with red plush seats
They're crawling with fleas and French actors
I see that even more of the audience are having trouble

It's a plague of fleas
It's driving me mad
All this scratching!
My head feels as if a Frenchman's living inside
And if one Frenchman is controlling your brain
playing on it
manipulating it
then you can forget it
Have you ever seen or heard a modest French puppeteer?
I haven't!
You can be sure of it
They start their show with a marionette
that dances the can-can
That's nothing
Then a small army of chauvinist marionettes starts chanting
'Beauty will be convulsive or will not be at all'
(*He chants in crescendo*)
'La beauté sera convulsive ou ne sera pas' (Beauty will be
convulsive or not at all) (3)

My name is John Soup
I'm the servant of beauty
Of nothing else!
Why was I jigging up and down
and jumping around?
Am I a flea?
Am I a sucking parasite
on myself?
Like beauty nourishes itself
by devouring itself
Yes, I'm a flea!
We've found the culprit
I'm the plague
who has to get you under control!
Look here
That's me, ping, ping, ping...
In action in the flea-circus
Now I'm pulling a little carriage
And now I'm jumping again
Ping, ping, ping
There we are, I set the carousel going
See that?
Oh, I'm so fast!
Ping, ping, ping...
What am I going to do now?
Kick penalties
Missed! Ping, ping, ping...
Against the crossbar! Ping, ping, ping...

Against the post! Ping, ping, ping...
My intuition tells me I'm going to score this time
Ping, ping, ping...
A long run-up
Goal
Goooooooooaaaaaal!
We're off to Mexico!
Goooooooooaaaaaal!
My, that was a long time ago
I'm in the wrong era again
Jean Potage, I mean John Soup, keep calm
You mustn't make a fool of yourself
You're not a ringmaster
in one or other circus
who has to raise his voice
who has the drummers play
so that the audience wouldn't miss
a tricky but short pirouette by the trapeze artiste!
Think of your 'patron'
Monsieur est servi? (are you being served, sir?)
But then, my 'patron' sometimes confuses me
Bingo!
Mon franc est tombé (my penny's dropped)
My 'patron'
La beauté is a disorder too (beauty is a disorder too)
An assault on my fickleness
and on my appraising thoughts
Merci patron (thanks patron)
for making me understand
that occasionally
I have to have a rest from myself
And at a moment like that
I'm ready for it
simply cover my eyes with tape
I feel I could be a person
you could look right through
Completely transparent
If you watched attentively
you would only see two small spherical lenses
reflecting in the light
Lenses that can go extremely flat
So that I'm a telescope
Lenses that can go extremely round
So that I'm a microscope
My eyes, lenses of eternal clarity
I want to turn the world upside down
No, not really
Because you always see the world upside down

I want to put the world on its feet!
It's impossible to train fleas
But it is possible to pass them on to you
Perhaps I'm of the old school?
Do you know what sort of work my 'patron' does?
That gave you a start
Yes, he works too, like everyone
My 'patron', beauty
is a sort of benefactor
He repairs the disrupted relations
we have created
My 'patron' has the gleam
of truth
He is the source
that lights up
and radiates clarity
As a servant I am the source of intuitive knowledge
What is intuitive knowledge
without the light of the intellect
What is the servant of beauty
What am I
without that beauty?
If beauty needs me
I need beauty far, far more
to get on in life
to change life
to improve life
As a servant I'm a source of intuition
Intuition is blind
Beauty gives me eyes
I'm ready for it
to enter the void
I have activated
a vital intensity
My unique act is taking place
I am slowly becoming careful
Yes, it's happening
In some places I can see through myself
A little longer
Then only marionettes will be visible
Oh, it's remarkable
but fantastic
For some time now
I haven't made any footprints
Well, well... Is that because I washed my feet
with my own tears?
Yes, it's possible
Because I feel that my feet are relaxed

They're as light as a feather
I'm becoming increasingly transparent
My magic formula works
My breaking index is the same
as that of air
Just tape over my eyes
There we are
I'm invisible
My body is cold
from a supernatural emotion
And now I have to pull the tape off my eyes
And see!
I am only mirrors
Mirrors of the soul
I am only mirrors
that wish to preserve worlds of beauty
Can you see me floating?
Watch attentively
Alright, those twinkling stars aren't very big
I think no one can see me
I can come and float
amongst you
the audience
And give you even more fleas
Then you can all go home scratching
I'm certain of it
No one can see me
I can do what I like
What can I get up to now?
What's the most provocative thing
I can do?
Yes, because I can elude anything
Look, I don't leave any footprints
I can even elude beauty
Live without beauty?
Not be the servant of my 'patron'?
That would make me sad
Perhaps that's no bad thing
Then I would cry at appropriate moments
Wash my feet with my own tears
Then my footprints would never betray me
Jamais (never)
Does the ultimate freedom exist?
Does the ultimate beauty exist?
But yes, don't forget
Beauty is a parody
and everybody knows
that there is always yet another interpretation missing

Lead is a parody of gold, for instance
Do you know how many jokes there are about the French?
One, because the rest are all true!
My marionettes-à-fil are better (my puppets on a string
are better)
than the best French actors
Because they have a divine grace
that's unknown to the human body
My creations do not act
They hold a celebration
in honour of their own symbolic worth
They are disarming in their poignancy
But I see...
the noses of my marionettes
growing?
Are they lying?
Yes! My 'patron' is content
Beauty is believing
in the lie of the imagination
You heard
I only want to use
my invisibility
for a good cause
Ah, that sounds nicely old-fashioned
In the service of beauty
Monsieur est servi? (are you being served, sir?)
But something horrible is happening
I can see it in front of me
The audience
–you–
are not entranced
You're scoffing at my creations
and throwing rotten eggs and tomatoes
That's where your favourite spectacle lies
The scandal!
My marionettes are being publicly mocked
and arrested for subversive behaviour
They are being charged with witchcraft
They are being tortured until they admit their guilt
And before my very eyes
they are being burnt at the stake
Now it's enough!
I'll put my eyes
in my pockets
So I shan't see you anymore
Oh, forget it
Theatre is a parody
And everything one sees in the theatre

is a parody of something else
Or the same thing in a misleading form
The marionette, for example, is a parody of the actor
So Antoinette, who has the ball
is a parody of the chopped-off heads
of the audience here
A French revolution
that still has to take place

◆

ABOUT THE AUTHOR

Jan Fabre (b. Antwerp, 1958), a graduate of the Municipal
Institute of Decorative Arts and the Royal Academy of Fine
Arts, is considered one of the most innovative and versatile
artists of his day. Over the past twenty-five years, he has
produced works as a performance artist, theatre maker,
choreographer, opera maker, playwright, and visual artist.
Jan Fabre is renowned for expanding the horizons of every
genre to which he applies his artistic vision.

In the late 1970s, the still very young Jan Fabre caused a
sensation as a performance artist. His money performances
involved setting fire to bundles of money from the audience
in order to make drawings with the ashes. In 1982, the work
Het is theater zoals te verwachten en te voorzien was (This is
Theatre As It was To Be Expected and Foreseen) and two
years later *De macht der theaterlijke dwaasheden* (The Power
of Theatrical Madness) challenged the foundations of the
European theatre establishment. Since then, Jan Fabre has
grown to become one of the most versatile theatre artists
on the international stage. He continues to break with the
conventions of contemporary theatre by introducing his
concept of "real-time performance"--also called "living
installations." Fabre explores radical choreography as a
means of resurrecting classical dance.

Fabre has been writing his own plays since 1975, first performed in 1989. Each play reflects Fabre's vision of theatre
as total art form in which dialogue is on a par with other
elements such as dance, music, movement, performance,
stage design, and improvisation. Chaos and discipline,
repetition and madness, metamorphosis and the anonymous
are indispensable ingredients in Fabre's theatre.

In addition to age-old rituals and philosophical questions,
Fabre also deals with themes of violence, lust, beauty, and
erotica. The body, in all its forms, has been the subject of
his investigations since the early 1980s. Productions such as
Je suis sang, Tannhäuser, Angel of Death, and *Quando l'uomo
principale è una donna* have earned Fabre international
acclaim.

In 2007, Jan Fabre created *Requiem für eine Metamorphose*
for the Salzburg Festspiele, RuhrTriennale and the Vilnius
Festival. In the same year he created *I am a Mistake* in

collaboration with Chantal Akerman and Wolfgang Rihm for a selection of European concert houses.

In 2008, Fabre wrote the solo *Another Sleepy Dusty Delta Day* for the Croatian performer Ivana Jozic based on the legendary Bobbie Gentry hit, *Ode to Billy Joe*. *Orgy of Tolerance* (2009), an absurdist satire explores the boundaries of normality in a society where everything is available and for sale.

In 2010, Fabre wrote the third part of the trilogy for Dirk Roofthooft: *The Emperor of Loss, The King of Plagiarism* and *The Servant of Beauty* were performend both in Dutch and French. For the 25th anniversary of the Festival Romaeuropa, Jan Fabre further developed the dance solo *Preparatio Mortis*, performed by dancer Annabelle Chambon to organ music by composer and organist Bernard Foccroulle.

In January 2011, the new theatre-dance production *Prometheus-Landschaft II* will have its world première in the Kasser Theatre of the Montclair State University.

Over the years, Jan Fabre has also built up an exceptional oeuvre as a visual artist, which has earned him extensive international renown. He has been part of several important international exhibitions such as the Venice Biennial (1984, 1990 and 2003), Documenta in Kassel (1987 and 1992), the Sao Paolo Biennial (1991), the Lyon Biennial (2000), the Valencia Biennial (2001), and the Istanbul Biennial (1992 and 2001), solo exhibition at the Musée du Louvre in Paris (2008, *Angel of Metamorphosis*). *From the Cellar to the Attic. From the Feet to the Brain* at Kunsthaus Bregenz (2008), *From the Feet to the Brain* in Venice venue Arsenale Novissimo (2009), *Art kept me out of jail*. Performance installations by Jan Fabre 2001-2004-2008 at M HKA (2010) and *Alternative humanities: Jan Fabre & Katsura Funakoshi* at 21st Century Museum of Contemporary Art, Kanazawa (2010).

Jan Fabre's literary work at the same time illustrates his thinking on theatre: theatre as an all embracing work of art in which the word is given a well-considered functional place next to such parameters as dance, music, opera, performance elements and improvisation. The austerity with which Fabre uses the medium of the word forces him to make theatre in an innovative way. When other directors work on these plays, they too are unable to distil any kind of conventional theatre out of them. And in recent years Jan Fabre's plays have indeed been regularly performed by other companies.

For more information about Jan Fabre and his theatre company *Jan Fabre | Troubleyn* please visit: http://www.troubleyn.be

The Martin E. Segal Theatre Center (MESTC), is a non-profit center for theatre, dance and film affiliated with CUNY's Ph.D. Program in Theatre. The Center's mission is to bridge the gap between academia and the professional performing arts communities both within the United States and internationally. By providing an open environment for the development of educational, community-driven, and professional projects in the performing arts, MESTC is a home to theatre scholars, students, playwrights, actors, dancers, directors, dramaturges, and performing arts managers from the local and international theatre communities. Through diverse programming— staged readings, theatre events, panel discussions, lectures, conferences, film screenings, dance— and a number of publications, MESTC enables artists, academics, visiting scholars and performing arts professionals to participate actively in the advancement and appreciation of the entire range of theatrical experience. The Center presents staged readings to further the development of new and classic plays, lecture series, televised seminars featuring professional and academic luminaries, and arts in education programs, and maintains its long-standing visiting scholars-from-abroad program. In addition, the Center publishes a series of highly-regarded academic journals, as well as books, including plays in translation, written, translated and edited by leading scholars.

For more information, please visit
http://web.gc.cuny.edu/mestc

The Graduate Center, CUNY, of which the Martin E. Segal Theatre Center is an integral part, is the doctorate-granting institution of The City University of New York (CUNY). An internationally recognized center for advanced studies and a national model for public doctoral education, the school offers more than thirty doctoral programs, as well as a number of master's programs. Many of its faculty members are among the world's leading scholars in their respective fields, and its alumni hold major positions in industry and government, as well as in academia. The Graduate Center is also home to twenty-eight interdisciplinary research centers and institutes focused on areas of compelling social, civic, cultural, and scientific concerns. Located in a landmark Fifth Avenue building, The Graduate Center has become a vital part of New York City's intellectual and cultural life with its extensive array of public lectures, exhibitions, concerts, and theatrical events.

To find out more, please visit:
http://www.gc.cuny.edu

The Ph.D. Program in Theatre, The Graduate Center, CUNY, is one of the leading doctoral theatre programs in the United States. Faculty includes distinguished professors, holders of endowed chairs, and internationally recognized scholars. The program trains future scholars and teachers in all the disciplines of theatre research. Faculty members edit MESTC publications, working closely with the doctoral students in theatre who perform a variety of editorial functions and learn the skills involved in the creation of books and journals.

For more information on the program, please visit: http://web.gc.cuny.edu/theatre

The MESTC Publication Wing produces both journals and individual volumes. Journals include Slavic and Eastern European Performance (SEEP), The Journal of American Drama and Theatre (JADT), and Western European Stages (WES). Books include Four Melodramas by Pixérécourt (edited by Daniel Gerould and Marvin Carlson— both Distinguished Professors of Theatre at the CUNY Graduate Center), Contemporary Theatre in Egypt (which includes the translation of three plays by Alfred Farag, Gamal Maqsoud, and Lenin El-Ramley, edited by Marvin Carlson), The Heirs of Molière (edited and translated by Marvin Carlson), Seven Plays by Stanisław Ignacy Witkiewicz (edited and translated by Daniel Gerould), The Arab Oedipus: Four Plays (edited by Marvin Carlson), Theatre Research Resources in New York City (edited by Jessica Brater, Senior Editor Marvin Carlson), and Comedy: A Bibliography of Critical Studies in English on the Theory and Practice of Comedy in Drama, Theatre and Performance (edited by Meghan Duffy, Senior Editor Daniel Gerould). New publications include: BAiT-Buenos Aires in Translation: Four Plays (edited and translated by Jean Graham-Jones), roMANIA AFTER 2000: Five New Romanian Plays (edited by Saviana Stanescu and Daniel Gerould), Four Plays from North Africa (edited by Marvin Carlson), and Barcelona Plays: A Collection of New Plays by Catalan Playwrights (edited and translated by Marion Peter Holt and Sharon G. Feldman).

To find out more, please visit:
http://web.gc.cuny.edu/mestc/subscribe.htm